The Wensleydale Railway

by

Christine Hallas

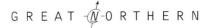

GREAT NORTHERN

Great Northern Books
PO Box 213, Ilkley, LS29 9WS

First published 1984 by Dalesman Books
Second edition 1991 by Leading Edge Press
Third edition 2002 by Great Northern Books
Fourth edition 2004
Published in association with The Wensleydale Railway plc

ISBN: 0 9544002 8 3

Designed by Blueprint Marketing Services Limited • Ilkley

Printed by The Amadeus Press Limited, Bradford, West Yorkshire.

A catalogue record for this book is available from the British Library

Contents

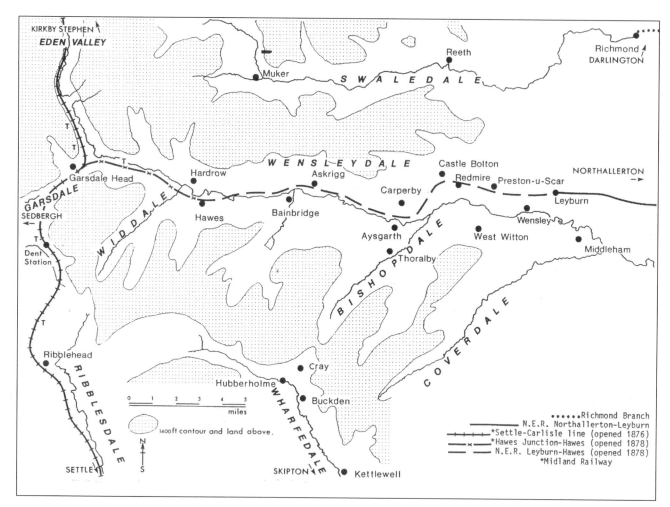

Railways constructed in the nineteenth century in the Wensleydale area.

Transport in Wensleydale before the railway

The winding and hilly roads in the dales may frustrate the car driver of today but for the dales people who lived before the coming of the railway they provided the lifeline of the community. The direction followed by the roads was dictated either by the contours and condition of the land or by the needs of farming and industry.

There were three main types of road in the dales. The major routes were the long established network that linked communities and that ran either from west to east along the main valley floors or north to south across the hills. This network was supplemented by drove roads, which were used to take flocks of sheep and herds of cattle to and from markets. Wensleydale was on a main droving route from Scotland to the urban centres in the south so stock frequently passed through the area and the dales people used the roads to move their own stock to market. It is estimated that, by the early 1870s, there were about 145,000 sheep journeys and about 40,000 cattle journeys made annually in and out of the Wensleydale and Swaledale area. Finally, the jagger roads formed the link between lead and coal mines and smelt mills. These roads then continued to the local centres from which lead was transported by cart to Stockton. The drove roads and jagger roads, which generally only carried goods on the hoof or by foot, often followed the most direct route and frequently traversed difficult terrain.

Roads for wheeled vehicles had to follow more gentle gradients but even these roads, in the mid-eighteenth century, were in poor condition and there was pressure to create turnpikes in the area. The road from Richmond, which passed through Wensleydale westwards to Lancaster, was reported in 1751 by petitioners for a turnpike to be:

so bad, ruinous, narrow and rocky that it is totally impassable at some Times of the Year for any Kind of Wheel Carriages …

The moorland road, which ran north from Askrigg in Wensleydale to Brough, was described in the late eighteenth century as 'fit only for a goat to travel'. When Lord Torrington travelled on this road in 1794 he claimed that it took him seven hours to travel the 20 miles from Barnard Castle to Askrigg. Lord Torrington also noted that the roads became virtually impassable in the depths of winter, effectively bringing to a standstill communication between the two dales. Despite the bad roads the dales people managed to travel for most of the year throughout Wensleydale and over the watersheds to Swaledale in the north and to Wharfedale in the south. As a result of the 1751 petitions an Act was passed which established a Turnpike Trust to link Richmond and Lancaster via Wensleydale. This Act marked the beginning of a long line of bills and acts which were to affect the road and the future rail system of Wensleydale. As with their railway counterparts who were to come later, the 175 petitioners for the 1751 Act claimed that the improved road would help the economy of Wensleydale to thrive and that the turnpike would gain a respectable revenue from the tolls.

However, as was to be expected given the lack of high demand locally, the tolls received in Wensleydale were not high. There were six toll bar sites in Wensleydale, at Redmire, Ballowfield, Askrigg, Brakenbar, Bainbridge and, from 1795, Hawes. These toll bars did not operate all at the same time but some were the result of re-siting. In 1773 the total tolls collected in Wensleydale amounted to £145. By 1844 tolls had risen to £172 but by 1860 they had declined to £137. Given that the turnpike mortgage was

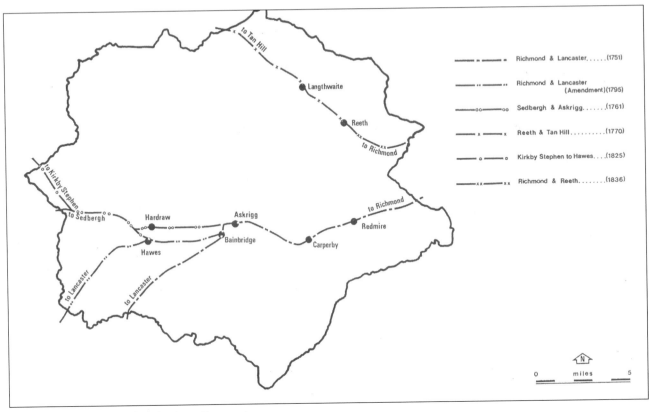

— — · —	Richmond & Lancaster	(1751)
— — ·· —	Richmond & Lancaster (Amendment)	(1795)
—oo— oo	Sedbergh & Askrigg	(1761)
—x— x	Reeth & Tan Hill	(1770)
—o— o	Kirkby Stephen to Hawes	(1825)
—xx— xx	Richmond & Reeth	(1836)

Wensleydale and Swaledale Turnpike roads.

£5,800 in 1795 and in the early nineteenth century the Turnpike Trust had a 'floating debt' of £751, it is likely that the Trust would have produced little surplus. Like the railway that was to follow, the Trust was built on optimistic speculation rather than sound economics. The Wensleydale turnpike continued to operate until 1868 when the Trust was terminated by an Act closing all turnpikes in the country. It had survived for only 117 years but this was longer than the railway, which was to follow.

Several other turnpike trusts were established in the area between 1770 and 1836. In 1770 a short turnpike road was constructed from Reeth in Swaledale via Arkengarthdale to connect with the Brough/Scotch Corner road. The principal reason for constructing this road was to exploit the Tan Hill coal pits and the lead mines in the area.

In an attempt to improve communications westwards from Wensleydale to the wool producing area around Kendal, and probably due partly to the influence of the

Richmond and Lancaster Trust, a turnpike from Askrigg to Sedbergh was authorized by Act in 1761. Turnpiking this area was further extended when in 1825 the road from Kirkby Stephen to Gayle on the outskirts of Hawes was authorized to be turnpiked.

The final turnpike act to affect the area was in 1836 when a ten-mile stretch of road between Richmond and Reeth was authorized. The lead mining interests in Swaledale had promoted the new road in 1821 to provide a cart route to carry lead from the dale. It was anticipated that, in addition to lead, stone and lime would also be exported and that the back carriage would bring corn, timber, coal and other goods into the dale.

Public Transport

Although most forms of road transport were private, some public transport was available in Wensleydale for at least part of the nineteenth century. This encouraged both local people and visitors to travel in and out of the area.

Prior to 1844 the Exmouth Coach Company had run a limited service in Wensleydale. In 1844 the Wensleydale Mail Company (which also carried passengers) took over the service and collected post from several centres in Wensleydale. By 1845 the coach service was extended to run from Leyburn to Northallerton railway station and in July 1845 a coach service was established on three days a week to run westwards to Sedbergh and Kendal during the summer months. Thus, not only was the Lake District accessible from the main railway line to the east but, as the coach travelled via Bedale, Middleham, Leyburn, Hawes and Sedbergh, these places could also be visited with relative ease.

In the late 1850s other forms of public transport, such as stage wagons and omnibuses, were run eastward to link with the railway station at Leyburn. A Hawes hotelier attempted to attract more visitors to the upper dale by placing the following advertisement in the *Richmond and Ripon Chronicle* in 1858:

T. Wetherill & Co. proprietors of the White Hart, Hawes, inform tourists and the public in general that they will run an omnibus every Monday and Friday between Hawes and Leyburn … This is an opportunity which has been rarely afforded to tourists who are wishful to visit the salubrious neighbourhood of Wensleydale.

The omnibus service was discontinued during winter but commenced again in March arriving at Leyburn on Mondays in time to catch the noon train, having left Hawes, seventeen miles away at 8.30 a.m. Friday was Leyburn market day and in order to accommodate local people the coach departed Hawes at 7 a.m. on Fridays to arrive some three hours later in good time for the market. Unfortunately, the omnibus venture was not a success and in 1861 the following advertisement appeared in the *Chronicle:*

The omnibus will not run between Hawes and Leyburn this season. N.B. Omnibus for sale, apply the owner, Thomas Wetherill.

Although the omnibus service survived only for a few years, dales people were able to travel by wheeled vehicle by using the more basic and cheaper facilities offered by carriers.

The carrier network in Wensleydale was vitally important to the industry and commerce of the area. There were specialist carriers, such as those who transported lead and coal or who collected farm produce to take to markets outside the dale, but there were also general carriers, who both linked the communities within the dales and transported goods in and out of the area.

Most of the carriers in the area operated from towns or villages which had, or had had, a market function and the most frequent journeys undertaken were to other places in the dales. Prior to the arrival of the main line railways in the

Carts collecting coal at Tan Hill coal pits, early twentieth century. (Author's collection)

1840s, regular carrier services were established to such places as Leeds, York, Stockton, Kendal, Lancaster, and Manchester. The dales people also used the services of long-haul carriers who plied their trade via Wensleydale from the North East to Lancashire.

Carriers were, therefore, very important particularly before the railway arrived. For example, in the 1820s over 30 carrier services per week were run in Wensleydale. The opening of the railway did not end the carrier trade in the dale. After a brief decline in 1879 the number of carrier services in upper Wensleydale had increased to their former level by the 1890s as more remote places were linked with the market town of Hawes.

In neighbouring Swaledale the number of carrier journeys increased significantly between 1823 and 1879 reflecting the use of carriers to Richmond station and to the Wensleydale railway. In the absence of a railway in Swaledale, the number of carrier journeys remained high in the 1890s, at 20 per week, and continued so into the twentieth century.

Although carriers provided a frequent and efficient network of transport in Wensleydale, when the chance of building a railway in the dale was first discussed in the 1840s most dales people greeted the scheme with enthusiasm. Some people recognised that if the dales were going to survive in the vibrant and technologically advanced world of Victorian England they would need a speedy form of transport. Other people undoubtedly wished for a railway in their area just because it was a new invention.

In the event the wish for a railway took a long time in coming to fruition.

2 Proposed railways in Wensleydale

In the mid-nineteenth century the people of Wensleydale lived for nearly 40 years in eager anticipation of a railway to serve their community. They recognised that it would bring a complete change of lifestyle and the change might not be always beneficial. This attitude was summarised in *The Wensleydale Advertiser*, a local newspaper, in 1846:

Thus, poor Wensleydale, which has so long been accounted one of the most quiet and peaceful vales in England must now doubtless become the scene of busy trade and tumult.

The schemes of the 1840s failed but from that date renewed speculation occurred at intervals, generally coinciding with the national booms in railway building. Many proposals were promulgated during the decades of the 1860s and 1880s, with a final flurry of speculation occurring at the turn of the century and petering out on the eve of the First World War.

After the plethora of proposals in the 1840s many subsequent schemes were merely revivals of previously abandoned plans. Some of the ideas were entirely fanciful but others were more feasible. Had national economic factors remained favourable a line most probably would have been built the length of Swaledale, and Wensleydale might well have enjoyed a rail connection southwards into Wharfedale.

Despite the wild claims of the promoters none of the proposed lines, including the one finally constructed, were likely to have been very profitable.

It is worth noting that each bill placed before Parliament was required to include a book of references and detailed plans of the route. The book of references listed land over which the proposed railway was to pass and named each landowner, lessee and occupier involved in the proposal. If the bill was authorised by Parliament there followed the lengthy process of negotiation settlements with each landowner. Over even a relatively short distance this could involve many individuals. For example, one scheme in the 1860s included a 16-mile stretch of line between Hardrow (near Hawes) and Leyburn. The line passed over land owned by 58 individual landowners, including the four extensive Wensleydale estates of Lord Bolton, The Earl of Wharncliffe, Lord Wensleydale, and Lady Vyner.

Each Scheme, therefore, involved detailed planning and discussion before it was presented to Parliament but it was only after authorisation that the hard bargaining really began. Local diarists attest to the controversies which arose over the settlement proposals of the North Eastern Railway (N.E.R.) and Midland Railway Companies when they eventually obtained acts authorising their lines in Wensleydale.

Proposals of the 1840s

The 1840s was the first and greatest period of railway promotion. The railway mania of this decade reached its national peak in 1846-7. During 1846 a capital of nearly £38m was raised by railway companies and by 1847 over 250,000 men were employed in the construction of 6,455 miles of railway.

Proposed railways in Wensleydale

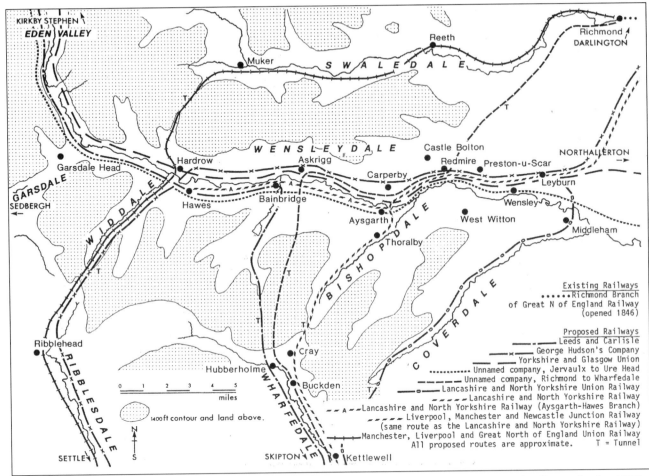

Proposed railways in the 1840s.

Wensleydale and the surrounding area did not escape unscathed from the speculators as had been hoped by some local people.

We had for years flattered ourselves with, as it has now proved, the delusive idea, that our valley presented *engineering difficulties to the formation of a Railway, which no public company would expend either its ingenuity or its funds to surmount. But we, last spring, found ourselves seriously mistaken. (The Wensleydale Advertiser, 1845)*

As the trunk lines were being extended northwards, by the Lancaster and Carlisle Railway Company to the west and the Great North of England Railway Company to the east, railway promoters sought suitable areas through which to construct links between the two systems. Wensleydale with its west-east alignment and relatively broad valley floor proved to be an attractive locality for many speculative schemes.

The railway surveyors descended upon the dale and busily staked out the proposed route with the coloured flags. In autumn 1845, *The Wensleydale Advertiser* reported:

Scarcely a day has elapsed in which the astonished natives have not been scared from their propriety by the apparition of numerous surveyors and their assistants, armed at all points with theodolites, levels, chains and flags.

The 'Traffic Takers' arrived and, to the amusement of local people, proceeded to keep watch day and night and count all vehicles on every road. One bemused resident, when asked the purpose of his journey, replied that he had "Com fra' haam an' am going back tu 't". A mischievous commentator noted that the railway personnel were having difficulty in "making an accurate return of asses (quadruped and biped) and the number of cats who made night excursions has occasioned sore perplexity"! In the sceptical opinion of some locals the traffic taking was useless as many native travellers would not avail themselves of the new mode of transport even if it were provided.

The editor of *The Wensleydale Advertiser* attempted to clarify the mixed feelings about the railway proposals through the columns of his newspaper. On the one hand he waxed lyrical about the impending invasion:

Alas, poor Wensleydale! Who can tell the changes thou art now doomed to experience! No longer wilt thou remain that secluded and peaceful district – the envied residence of retired happiness and contentment! Henceforth, the

echoes of thy hills must resound to the shrill whistle of the steam engines, and thou must shortly become united to the busy world beyond their boundaries.

On the other hand, the editor foresaw many economic advantages for the area. Dairy products would be quickly sold to the industrial West Riding, manufacturers would establish businesses in the dale providing work for local people, mineral wealth would be exploited and

the frequent and ready transit will bring us hosts of visitors, who, but for a Railway, would never see Wensleydale or its beauties; and this event may prove some return for the benefits of which it [Wensleydale] may be, by the same means deprived.

By the mid 1840s a profusion of speculative schemes had been presented, many of which were later modified and further complicated by amalgamations of companies with proposals following similar routes. In the autumn of 1845 at least nine schemes affecting the area had been announced and several modified plans were deposited for the consideration of the next Parliament. Many of these plans were later withdrawn and only four railway companies, York and Carlisle; Yorkshire and Glasgow Union; Liverpool, Manchester and Newcastle Junction; and Lancashire and North Yorkshire actually presented bills in the 1846 Parliamentary session. Even these four companies were subject to further amalgamation as the session progressed. Had all the schemes come to fruition twenty railway bridges would have spanned the Ure between Leyburn and Hawes.

The nine original schemes fall into two main groups, those seeking to connect the area south of Wensleydale with the north east and those proposing to link the area to the south with the north west.

The Manchester, Liverpool and Great North of England Union Railway Company (later the Northumberland and

Old Faithful No 67345 on Mossdale Head Viaduct just east of Garsdale in the early 1950s. The rugged landscape is typical of that through which the railway had to pass on its route to Leyburn. (N.E. Stead collection)

Lancashire Junction Railway Company) prepared a grandiose scheme to connect

by the shortest possible communication Manchester and the Manufacturing District of the West Riding of Yorkshire with the mining districts of Durham and Northumberland and the important Towns and Ports of Liverpool and Newcastle.

The proposed railway, if built, would commence near Settle and proceed in a north-easterly direction to Hawes. The route would continue, via a three-mile tunnel, into Swaledale and follow the River Swale to Richmond where it would meet the proposed branch line of the Great North of England Railway. The company maintained that the returns derived from the local traffic of the lead mining industry would alone make the line profitable but, in addition, the line would carry many passengers and facilitate the movement of substantial coal traffic from Durham to Settle and North Lancashire. The price of coal at Settle was twenty shillings per ton but the company forecast that with a good rail link the price would fall to as little as eight shillings per ton. There was much local interest in the scheme. Several members of the provisional committee were from the area and the Swaledale and Wensleydale Banking Company was one of ten banks involved. The scheme, however, proved too ambitious and was withdrawn in late 1845.

An unidentified company also proposed to connect the two dales. The scheme involved driving a tunnel from Swaledale, west of Richmond, southwards to emerge near Redmire in Wensleydale. The line would then proceed in a westerly direction before turning due south at Askrigg to leave Wensleydale via another tunnel under Addleborough! Needless to say, this scheme was quickly abandoned.

The famous Railway King, George Hudson, briefly proposed to construct a line from Catterick southwards to Hunton then westwards through Wensleydale to Hawes

before leaving the dale in a south westerly direction via a tunnel of 3,344 yards under Widdale Head into Ribblesdale. The plan failed to come to fruition.

The Lancashire and North Yorkshire Union Railway Company proposed to build a line which would commence from a junction with the intended line of the Leeds and Bradford Extension Railway at Elslack near Skipton. The proposed route ran north through Wharfedale passed by tunnel under Great Whernside and, after emerging in Coverdale, continued to Middleham. The wide Ure valley floor would be spanned with a large embankment to enable the line to cross from Middleham to Spennithorne and continue into Leyburn. Shortly after announcing this scheme the company amalgamated with the Lancashire and North Riding Junction Railway Company to become the Lancashire and North Yorkshire Railway Company. The former plan was abandoned in favour of a 3,850 yard tunnel from Cray near Buckden in Wharfedale to Bishopdale. The proposed line would then proceed to Aysgarth Falls, which would be spanned by a bridge, before swinging eastwards to Leyburn and on to Catterick where it would join the intended Richmond Branch line of the Great North of England Railway. A branch line was to be constructed to serve upper Wensleydale between Aysgarth and Hawes.

A further company, the Liverpool, Manchester and Newcastle-upon-Tyne Junction Railway, deposited plans for a similar route but common sense and hard economics prevailed and discussions were entered into with the Lancashire and North Yorkshire Company. The two companies agreed to promote a joint line, following approximately the same route as that of Lancashire and North Yorkshire Company, to be called the Liverpool, Manchester and Newcastle-upon-Tyne Railway. Each company would retain its separate identity and it was eventually agreed that the Liverpool, Manchester and Newcastle-upon-Tyne Junction Railway Company would construct the branch line to Hawes.

Several proposals involved schemes for crossing the dale from a south easterly to a north westerly direction. Another unidentified company presented plans for a line to run into Wensleydale via Jervaulx Abbey, follow the Ure to its head and proceed to Kirkby Stephen. The Yorkshire and Glasgow Union Railway Company also proposed a similar route which would commence near Bedale, travel westward through Wensleydale on the northern bank of the Ure before swinging north-westwards via Kirkby Stephen to Clifton near Penrith, to join the Lancaster and Carlisle Railway. The promoters claimed that this railway would not only connect the two trunk routes but would serve to promote the trade of Leyburn and the agricultural interests of the surrounding districts.

Later in 1845 this same company established a small office in Hawes and stated that it and no other independent company should construct a branch line from Hawes southwards to Settle to join the North Western Railway. This jealous statement was possibly in response to the plans of the Leeds and Carlisle Railway Company. Their proposed route was from Hubberholme in upper Wharfedale via a tunnel of 5,849 yards to emerge in Cragdale and follow the shore of Semerwater before descending into Wensleydale at Bainbridge. The line would then swing westwards to Hawes and follow a similar route to that of the Yorkshire and Glasgow Union towards Kirkby Stephen. After discussions these two companies agreed to amalgamate and in 1846 the Leeds and Carlisle withdrew its plans in favour of the Yorkshire and Glasgow Union proposal.

Another company, the York and Carlisle, deposited proposals for a route in the area, though not through Wensleydale. However, during the Parliamentary hearing in May 1846 it announced plans to amalgamate with the Yorkshire and Glasgow Union under the title of Northern Counties Union Railway Company. The companies would retain responsibility for their separate lines but a joint railway would be constructed where possible. In September 1846, engineers from both companies were dispatched to jointly stake out the first section of the line between Constable Burton and Carperby and to prepare a proposal for an amended bill to be placed before the 1847 session of Parliament.

By the early autumn of 1846, therefore, all the schemes of the previous eighteen months had been whittled down to two proposals; that of the Northern Counties Union Railway Company whose route followed the Ure from east to west before swinging northwards to Kirkby Stephen; and that of the Liverpool, Manchester and Newcastle upon Tyne Railway Company which proposed to construct a railway from Wharfedale to the north east with a branch line from Aysgarth to Hawes. The latter company agreed with withdraw the branch line proposal if the Northern Counties Union commenced construction of their section of the line between Aysgarth and Hawes before 31 December 1847.

Both schemes enjoyed local support, but the Northern Counties Union proposals appeared to be particularly popular. When the villagers of Askrigg received the news in July 1846 that the Northern Counties bill had been authorised, church bells were rung and a band paraded in the main street. There were similar celebrations in other villages along the proposed route. The inhabitants of Wensleydale were becoming more accustomed to the idea of a railway in their midst but they still regarded the prospect with mixed feelings. However, there was no denying the benefits of improved communication and enhanced trade:

Railways and coaches place us almost within speaking distance of the large towns and to such ... as can snatch a day of innocent recreation we heartily cry "Come!" (The Wensleydale Advertiser, 1846)

But what if the visitors were not innocent? Fears grew that the visitors and particularly the railway navvies would be lawless and demands were made for new "lock-ups" to be built at Leyburn, Askrigg and Hawes in readiness for the invasion. One local correspondent suggested that the two railway companies employ a staff of police to control their labourers:

If no steps are to be taken, to avert or prohibit the misdoings of these rude, illiterate, misguided men, we cannot complain if the ruthless arm of the desperado fall heavily on our heads, ... if our properties should be invaded and plundered, - if our females should become the victims of violence, or our dwellings the prey of the burglar. (The Wensleydale Advertiser, 1847)

Public pressure prevailed and tenders were invited for a new "lock-up" at Leyburn. The building, containing two cells, was completed in 1847 but was not required for railway navvies for several years, as neither the hopes nor the fears concerning a Wensleydale railway were realised at this time.

In January 1848 the authorised line of the Liverpool, Manchester and Newcastle-upon-Tyne Railway was abandoned and the company later dissolved due to lack of finance. The survival of the Northern Counties Union railway was also in doubt. The directors reaffirmed that they hoped to open the Wath to Leyburn section in summer 1848, but stated that they did not contemplate an extension of the railway beyond Leyburn. During 1848, some work on the Wath to Leyburn section commenced but was soon abandoned leaving Wensleydale without any immediate prospect of a railway. However, in 1853 the Bedale and Leyburn Railway Company was formed and with some support from the new North Eastern Railway Company opened their line between Bedale and Leyburn in May 1856. The new railway connected with the York, Newcastle and Berwick line from Northallerton to Bedale which had been authorised in 1846 and was completed in 1955.

The people of upper Wensleydale had to wait much longer as one commentator prophetically stated in 1848:

Doubtless we shall witness a great many New Year's Days ere the promoters will be able to land a London Cockney at the station house on the gigantic rocks of Hardrow Scar. (The Wensleydale Advertiser, 1848)

Proposals of the 1860s

Despite the failure of the 1840s proposals, the success of the Bedale and Leyburn Company meant that a railway was within reach of Wensleydale and this augured well for future schemes. Further, in 1858, after the Bedale and Leyburn Company encountered financial difficulties, the N.E.R. took over the line, thus giving a large company a firm interest in the area.

The 1860s saw an upsurge in railway promotion throughout the country and once again Wensleydale experienced a spate of schemes, many of which had close similarities to those presented in the 1840s.

In autumn 1864 the North of England Union Railway Company deposited a series of plans for a link from Settle to the north east. Three of the proposals directly affected Wensleydale. The first was to construct a line from Settle Junction to follow a route similar to that of the present Settle-Carlisle line as far as Ribblehead. The proposed line would then proceed in a north-easterly direction through Widdale to Hardrow before swinging eastwards along the northern slopes of Wensleydale to Leyburn, a total distance of 37 miles. The second proposal was for a line of 20 miles to be constructed from the first line, just west of Leyburn, to follow a north-easterly direction to Darlington. A short branch line westwards from Hardrow to Sedbergh was also proposed.

The Skipton and Wharfedale and Leyburn Railway Company also deposited plans in autumn 1864 for

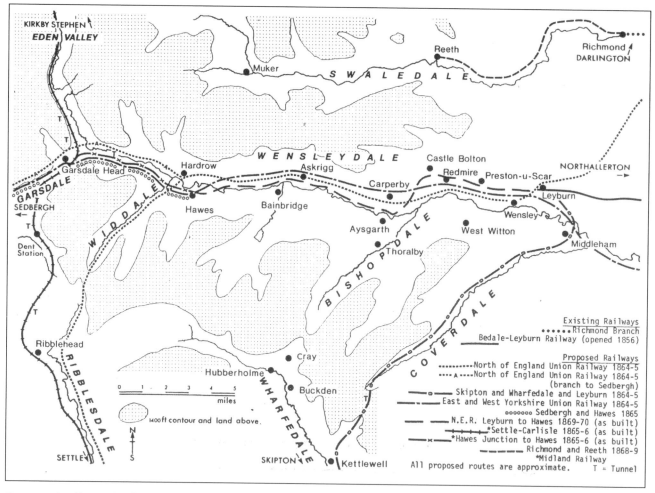

KIRKBY STEPHEN
EDEN VALLEY

Muker

S W A L E D A L E

Reeth

Richmond
DARLINGTON

NORTHALLERTON
→

W E N S L E Y D A L E

Hardrow
Askrigg
Castle Bolton
Redmire
Preston-u-Scar

GARSDALE
Garsdale Head

Carperby

Leyburn

SEDBERGH
←

Hawes
Bainbridge

Wensley

Dent
Station

W
I
D
D
A
L
E

Aysgarth

West Witton

B
I
S
H
O
P
D
A
L
E

Middleham

Thoralby

Ribblehead

Cray

C
O
V
E
R
D
A
L
E

Hubberholme

R
I
B
B
L
E
S
D
A
L
E

0 1 2 3 4 5
miles

1400 ft contour and land above.

N
S

W
H
A
R
F
E
D
A
L
E

Buckden

Existing Railways
•••••• Richmond Branch
Bedale-Leyburn Railway (opened 1856)

Proposed Railways
····· North of England Union Railway 1864-5
··A·· North of England Union Railway 1864-5
       (branch to Sedbergh)
——○— Skipton and Wharfedale and Leyburn 1864-5
——□— East and West Yorkshire Union Railway 1864-5
○○○○○ Sedbergh and Hawes 1865
———— N.E.R. Leyburn to Hawes 1869-70 (as built)
—+—+— *Settle-Carlisle 1865-6 (as built)
—×—×— *Hawes Junction to Hawes 1865-6 (as built)
— — — Richmond and Reeth 1868-9
       *Midland Railway
All proposed routes are approximate.   T = Tunnel

SETTLE

SKIPTON

Kettlewell

Proposed railways in the 1860s.

consideration in the 1865 parliamentary session. These plans involved constructing a railway from Kettlewell in Wharfedale via a tunnel of nearly 2,000 yards into Coverdale and on to Middleham from where it would proceed to join the Bedale and Leyburn railway near Leyburn. The promoters hoped the line would provide a vital link between the iron producing area near Middlesbrough and the port of Liverpool. The proposal was later abandoned partly due to opposition from the N.E.R.

A further scheme was presented by the East and West Yorkshire Union Railway Company, which proposed a line from Melmerby via Masham into Wensleydale. The line would then proceed in a westerly direction through Garsdale to connect with the North Western system near Sedbergh. The proposal was later modified to terminate at Hawes and was renamed the Hawes and Melmerby Railway. The scheme appears to have enjoyed much local support. A tourist booklet on Wensleydale by George Hardcastle included a detailed plan of the route which was to traverse the northern slopes of Wensleydale. Hardcastle commented that the scheme would be of inestimable advantage to upper Wensleydale which until then had been isolated from the world. The mineral and agricultural resources would be tapped and tourism become important.

I almost envy the thousands of wanderers who may follow me into Wensleydale, the ready access which this railway extension will give them to almost every scene and object of interest.

The Hawes and Melmerby Railway had a further advantage in the active financial backing of the N.E.R. and an Act authorising the line was passed in 1865.

Another scheme which affected Wensleydale was that of the Sedbergh and Hawes Railway Company which in 1866 proposed to construct a 15-mile link between the authorised Hawes terminus of the Hawes and Melmerby Railway and the Lancaster, Carlisle and Ingleton branch of the London and North Western Railway near Sedbergh. The scheme was later abandoned.

During the mid 1860s the Midland Railway Company signed an agreement with the North of England Union Railway to supersede their earlier proposal. The Midland Company would construct a line between Settle and Carlisle with a branch line to Hawes from a junction at Garsdale. An Act for this scheme was obtained in 1866. The prospect of a through line for Wensleydale now looked promising but yet more problems loomed on the horizon.

In 1868 the Midland Company, finding the costs of the Settle-Carlisle line exorbitant, applied to abandon the whole project including the Hawes branch. Had the application been successful it is probable that the Hawes and Melmerby scheme, backed by the N.E.R., would also have been abandoned. Fortunately for Wensleydale, Parliament refused to ratify the abandonment bill and construction of the Settle-Carlisle line continued.

Further problems arose: due to financial difficulties the Hawes and Melmerby line was postponed and later abandoned when a more modest N.E.R. scheme was authorised to connect the proposed Midland branch line at Hawes with the existing N.E.R. terminus at Leyburn. The new 16 mile N.E.R. line was to follow a similar route to that of the Hawes and Melmerby Railway though at a lower altitude. It appears that the N.E.R. were aware that the railway would never be particularly profitable but were prepared to construct the line in order to prevent competitors from encroaching into their area.

During the 1860s attempts were made by local people in Swaledale to attract railway promoters to their area. John Ward, writing in *Methodism in Swaledale*, in 1865, voiced the feeling of many:

Two things at present make against the material prosperity of the dales people viz., the comparative unproductiveness of the lead mines, and also the want of railway accommodation, the nearest station [to Reeth] being Leyburn eight miles distant and Richmond, ten and a half miles.

Ward continued with the comment that these factors had forced people to leave the dale in search of employment. Despite this concern only one independent company deposited plans for a railway in Swaledale. The proposal was to construct a ten mile link between Richmond and Reeth and this was authorised by Parliament in 1869. But the now familiar problem of lack of finance overtook the scheme and Leyburn remained the nearest station for the people of upper Swaledale.

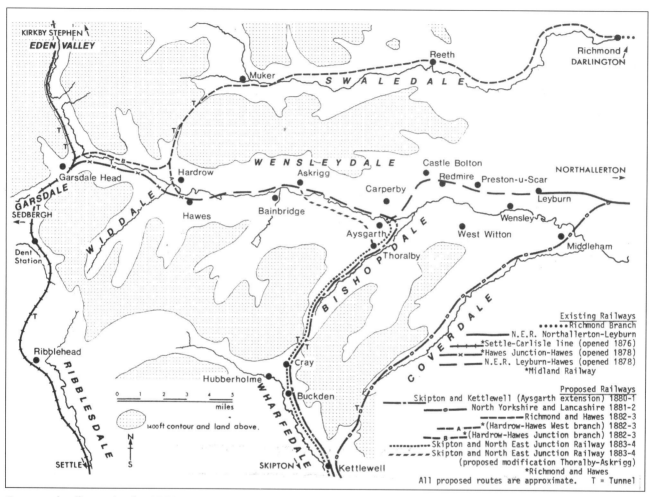

Proposed railways in the 1880s.

Proposals of the 1880s

As detailed in the following chapter, the Wensleydale line from Leyburn to Hawes Junction at Garsdale opened in 1878 but this did not end railway speculation in the area. The 1880s saw yet another outburst of railway promotion and once again Wensleydale was affected, this time with particular interest focussing on a connection between Wharfedale and Wensleydale.

In November 1880, the Skipton and Kettlewell Railway Company deposited plans at the House of Lords Private Bills Office. The Company's intention was to extend the proposed line from Skipton to Kettlewell forward to Buckden and thence by a tunnel of 2,410 yards into Bishopdale and northwards eventually to cross the Ure and join the N.E.R. line west of Aysgarth station, a distance of nine miles. This plan was superseded in November 1883 by the Skipton and North East Junction Railway Company Bill which proposed a 17-mile route similar to the earlier one but which was to commence at Grassington, to enter a 3,000 yard tunnel east of the hamlet of Cray, and to pass through the village of Thoralby into Wensleydale.

These two proposals both involved constructing a bridge that would span the Ure at Aysgarth Falls. This led to an outcry of protest throughout the country. After the first proposal, an Aysgarth Defence Association was formed in 1881 which included such eminent persons as John Ruskin, L. Alma Tadema, William Morris, Edmund Gosse, Walter Besant and Ouida, the celebrated novelist. The Earl of Wharncliffe, who had a substantial estate in upper Wensleydale, was the Association's president. A booklet *The Railway Vandal at Aysgarth Force*, stated that the railway company proposed

to throw a railway bridge on brick skew arches, 80 feet above the bed of the river over High Force and [construct the line] through the wood and glen at the entrance of the Bear Park estate.

Potential dangers were foreseen for the unsuspecting horseman riding down the steep track to the falls:

What will be likely to happen ... when a puffing, screeching monster, vomiting fire, is suddenly seen in front, and high above the heads by horses?

Protest meetings were arranged and a lively correspondence about the proposals took place. Sir Frederick Leighton, President of the Royal Academy, noted that public opinion was rising in anger against those who were seeking to deface the natural beauties of the country in this way. Another correspondent described Aysgarth Falls as "the fairest spot in all Yorkshire, perhaps in all England" and another begged for "some corner of earth pure from the shriek of the steam engine and the noise of the rushing train".

Messrs. Agnew and Sons of Old Bond Street, London, exhibited J.M.W. Turner's *Aysgarth Falls* in order that people in the capital could see the beauty which was in imminent danger of being destroyed.

The pressure of protest continued and reached a peak in 1884 when Professor John Hales of London University stated that the proposed bridge was like inserting a page of Bradshaw in the midst of Spenser's *Faerie Queene*. Another objector referred to the promoters as barbarians who imagined "a tourist seeking enjoyment at Clapham Junction".

Ouida wrote prophetically to *The Times*:

If science have any of the skill it pretends to possess, so ugly, noisy, clumsy, and dangerous a method of locomotion as railways offer will, before 50 years more have passed, be superseded by some other invention.

In view of the outcry the promoters suggested a diversion, the line would continue on the south side of the Ure and cross at Worton to join the N.E.R. system at Askrigg. But this proposal led to further problems and due to a mixture of public pressure and economic factors the whole scheme was eventually abandoned leaving Aysgarth Falls undisturbed for the enjoyment of posterity.

A further scheme for a Wharfedale-Wensleydale link had been proposed in autumn 1881 by the North Yorkshire and Lancashire Railway. The Company hoped to provide a

High Falls, Aysgarth, with a drawing of the proposed railway viaduct of the 1880s superimposed in the background. (M. Kirby collection)

direct route between Lancashire and the north east and further maintained that Lancashire would be able to supply the dales with good quality cheap coal and other commodities. The proposed 33-mile line was to be constructed as an extension from an intended line between Hellifield and Grassington and was to pass from Wharfedale to Coverdale via a two-mile tunnel and join the N.E.R. Bedale-Leyburn line near Constable Burton. However, many doubted that the scheme would be of much economic advantage either as a link line or as a

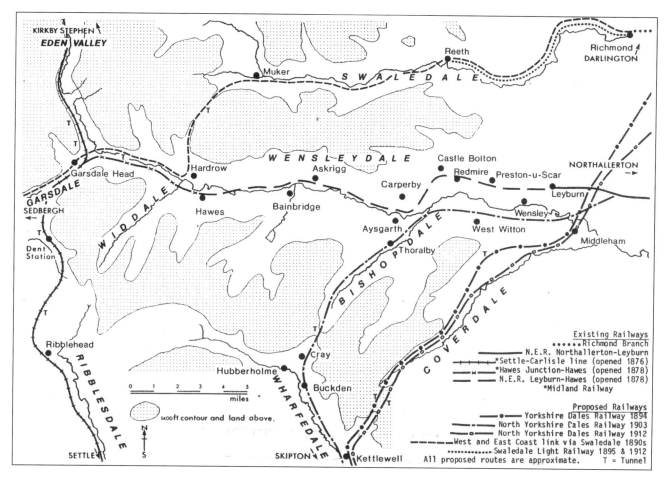

Final proposals.

21

carrier of commodities to the area and so the proposals were withdrawn. In response to the schemes promoted by its rivals the N.E.R. presented plans to provide links southwards but due to some local opposition and lack of capital the proposals were abandoned.

Further attempts were made in the 1880s to construct a railway in Swaledale which, it was hoped, would revive the ailing lead mining industry. The Richmond and Hawes Railway proposed a line westwards from Richmond via Marske and Reeth to the head of Swaledale, before swinging southwards to pass by two tunnels (1,504 yards and 563 yards) under Great Shunner Fell to emerge in Wensleydale. The proposed line then proceeded as two branches, one to connect with the main Midland Settle-Carlisle line a few miles distant at Garsdale Head and the other to join the Midland branch line west of Hawes. But, the scheme proved too ambitious and the required capital could not be raised so Swaledale remained without the prospect of a railway.

Final proposals

Speculative interest in the area was renewed towards the end of the nineteenth century when railway promoters again attempted to establish a link between Wharfedale and Wensleydale. The proposals had a now familiar ring to them. In November 1894 the Yorkshire Dales Railway Company deposited plans for a line to be constructed from Hetton via Wharfedale to Kettlewell before following the popular route of a tunnel (6,000 yards this time) under Great Whernside to emerge in Coverdale. The next section of the route was novel. After traversing the length of Coverdale the line would pass through a tunnel of 770 yards under the eastern spur of Penhill to emerge near Middleham. The line would then swing in a north-easterly direction to join the main N.E.R. line south of Darlington. A massive £1,750,000 of capital was required for this venture and, not surprisingly, the scheme failed through lack of subscription.

The promoters were not daunted and in 1903 the North Yorkshire Dales Railway Company presented another scheme. In this proposal the connecting tunnel of 3,100 yards was to be between Cray in upper Wharfedale and Bishopdale and the line would terminate at a junction with the N.E.R. Bedale-Leyburn line near Constable Burton. This plan also failed. A final attempt was presented in 1912 when the North Yorkshire Dales Railway Company proposed to construct a line along the 1894 route with the modifications of a 4,800 yard tunnel and a direct run north eastwards to cross the Bedale-Leyburn line at Harmby, to terminate at a junction with the N.E.R. Richmond branch near Scorton. Predictably the scheme failed leaving the small valleys of Bishopdale and Coverdale and the hills of upper Wharfedale undisturbed by the railway.

These years also saw the final attempts to construct a railway in Swaledale. An expensive proposal in the early 1890s to connect the west and east coast via Swaledale quickly failed, as did a scheme presented in 1895 to construct a light railway between Richmond and Reeth. However, in 1912 the prospect was more hopeful when the Swaledale Light Railway Order was granted, authorising the construction of a ten mile single line between Richmond and Reeth. The estimated construction cost was £40,307 but despite much local interest, and an agreement with the N.E.R. concerning rolling stock, the required capital could not be raised and the scheme was finally abandoned in 1922. The people of upper Swaledale had to resign themselves to crossing the watershed into Wensleydale and travelling on the only railway to be constructed out of all the speculative proposals of the previous decades.

3 The building of the Wensleydale Railway

As previously stated, the N.E.R., concerned to protect areas which it considered to be its territory, sought to extend its Northallerton to Leyburn line to Hawes to provide a connection with Midland railway system to the west of the Pennines. The Company's proposal for a railway line between Leyburn and Hawes was authorised by Act of Parliament on 4 July, 1870.

The Darlington and Stockton Times described the new route that was to cover a distance of 16 miles 195 yards, as follows:

the branch from Leyburn to Hawes, in order to avoid obstacles, proceeds in a rather circuitous line up the dale. Commencing at the present station at Leyburn, it passes underneath the road to Middleham, winds along the hillside to the south of the village [Leyburn], crosses the Wensley road, skirts the base of the cliff known as the Shawl, and proceeding onward passes near the lead mine at Keld Head, leaves Bolton Hall a little to the south, touches at the village of Redmire and a little further on passes in front of the grim-looking ruins of Bolton Castle. Thence the line, taking a south-westerly direction runs to the village of Carperby, passes close by Aysgarth Falls, and continues on past Bear Park, [towards] Nappa Hall through an extensive rabbit warren known as "Nappa Warren", and onto Askrigg, Bowbridge, Bainbridge, and further on it crosses the Ure and proceeds thence to Hawes.

The line followed approximately the 600 foot contour between Leyburn and Aysgarth after which it climbed to reach 700 feet at Askrigg and 750 feet at Hawes.

Five new stations were to serve the N.E.R. line west of Leyburn: at Wensley, Redmire, Aysgarth, Askrigg and Hawes. All, with the exception of Hawes, were situated either completely outside or on the outskirts of the community they served. Wensley station was equidistant between the village of Wensley and Preston-under-Scar though convenient for Bolton Hall, the seat of Lord Bolton. Aysgarth station was situated to the north of the River Ure in Carperby township and was equidistant between Carperby and Aysgarth villages. These arrangements did not please everyone. The residents of Bainbridge unsuccessfully petitioned the N.E.R. directors for a station to be constructed near their village at Yore Bridge instead of the proposed site at Askrigg.

Redmire station c1900. (WRA collection)

The Midland Company branch line was five miles 1,577 yards in length and climbed steadily from Hawes to reach a height of over 1,000 feet at Hawes Junction. This short stretch ran through beautiful but rugged countryside and required several minor engineering feats including a five-arched viaduct to straddle Widdale Beck, a four-arched viaduct over Mossdale Beck and a short tunnel of 245 yards near Mossdale Head. Under the terms of the 1866 Act the Midland Company agreed to construct a small station at the junction of the branch with the Settle-Carlisle line. This station was originally designated "Hawes Junction", but at the turn of the century the name was changed to "Hawes Junction and Garsdale" and later, in 1933, renamed "Garsdale (for Hawes)".

The lines of the two companies met at Hawes where a joint station was to be built. The Midland Company agreed to undertake construction work and in 1876 submitted plans for the station to be built at an estimated cost of £4,760. The N.E.R. approved the plans and accepted liability for half the cost.

Although the Leyburn to Hawes line had been authorised in 1870 construction work did not commence until 1873. *The Darlington and Stockton Times* reported in February of that year.

The land plans are ready for being served with notices on all the landowners and plans for letting the works are also ready, and only waiting until the directors consider it desirable that they should be let, having regard to the state of the market for labour and materials.

In addition, there were problems to be resolved with some of the landowners. William Tomlinson, a substantial landowner near Aysgarth, objected that he was being offered only £1,335 for the purchase of land, which his adviser valued at £2,738. The dispute was taken to arbitration and a compromise figure of £1,985 was awarded. Another farmer objected that the railway company proposed to acquire some of his best hay meadows, contending that this would be to his economic disadvantage as already he had to buy extra hay for his stock. The land agent for the extensive Metcalfe estate in the vicinity of Hawes recorded several site meetings with company officials in an attempt to reach agreement on compensation for compulsory land purchase. The Midland Company began negotiations with landowners in the late 1860s and, by 1869, was acquiring land and making compensation payments. The Midland also encountered problems and in the case of both companies some settlements were not agreed until the late 1870s. However, the most pressing problems were resolved and in November 1873 *The Richmond and Ripon Chronicle* reported that construction had commenced on the N.E.R. line, though at a leisurely pace. It appears that even by 1875 the line had been laid only to a point eight miles west of Leyburn.

The final authorisation in 1870 had provided for a single line from Leyburn to Hawes with double line workings and sidings at each station. Messrs. Gibb and Son were appointed contractors for the line. Many bridges, cuttings and embankments were required to maintain the steady gradient from Leyburn and to accommodate the streams and roads traversing the line at different points. In addition, cattle walks had to be constructed where the railway separated the farmer from his grazing stock. Some of the cuttings necessitated the removal of many thousands of cubic yards of rock. One cutting was 22 feet deep, 880 yards long and required the removal of nearly 60,000 cubic yards of rock. Local quarries were used to provide the ballast to support the track.

Occasionally unusual discoveries were made. When the navvies were constructing the line immediately west of Askrigg a quantity of human bones were excavated from the foundation of an old bridge. Nearby, lengths of lead water pipes were unearthed leading from a spring to the site of Fors Abbey. A section of the pipe is preserved at the Dales Countryside Museum at Hawes.

Garsdale station circa 1950 on the Settle-Carlisle line. It was originally called Hawes Junction and renamed Garsdale (for Hawes) in 1933. Note the glass and iron canopy which has since been demolished. (N.E. Stead)

G5 0-4-4T No 67314 leaving Garsdale from the platform created specially for the Wensleydale Branch on the Settle-Carlisle line. (WRA collection)

The line was not built without physical cost. In February 1875, a young man was severely injured and lost his sight while attempting to blast a tree root in the path of the new line near Preston-under-Scar.

Another accident for which the construction works were held partly responsible occurred in June 1875. A Miss Pilkington, travelling from London to her family's country residence at Swinithwaite Hall near West Witton, telegraphed her father, a Blackburn manufacturer, from Leyburn that she had safely completed the train journey and would proceed the last few miles by carriage. As the young lady and her two maids were crossing a temporary, rickety wooden bridge over a deep railway cutting near Leyburn the carriage shaft broke. To avoid being hurled over the bridge the three women jumped out. The maids escaped with minor injuries but Miss Pilkington fractured her skull and died instantly.

As unexpected difficulties lengthened construction time

the costs rose. In the mid 1870s the estimated cost of the N.E.R. line was £211,000 but by 1878 the final cost was substantially higher at £233,251 or about £14,000 per mile. The cost of the Midland branch was even higher and may be conservatively estimated at £240,000 or £40,000 per mile for the single track.

There were other problems for the contractors who had to contend with thefts of materials that were placed along the line in preparation for construction. It appears that these were regarded as "fair game". In 1878 two men were discovered stealing lime belonging to the Midland Company from a truck near Hawes Junction. When apprehended they stated that they thought the lime belonged to the contractors and would not have considered taking it if they had realised it was the property of the Midland Company. The men were convicted of theft.

Until the arrival of the railway navvies, Wensleydale had had relatively little day-to-day contact with the outside world. The last major immigration had been the Viking settlement of the ninth century and, therefore, the social

Site of navvy settlement near Moorcock Inn where railway navvies lived – sometimes 23 to a hut. (Author's collection)

impact on the community of this latest (albeit temporary) immigration must have been considerable.

Unfortunately, there is no record of the numbers of labourers involved in the construction of the N.E.R. line but a substantial workforce must have been employed in the dale when the construction was at its peak in the mid 1870s. There is, however, some indication of the numbers involved in working on the Midland Settle-Carlisle line and the Hawes branch. The railway workers lived in settlements scattered along the length of the main line.

The community which supplied labour for the Garsdale section of the Settle-Carlisle line and the Hawes branch was based a few miles west of Hawes near the Moorcock Inn. In 1871 142 navvies, some with their dependants, lived in ten wooden huts. The numbers resident in each hut varied from 23 people to a hut accommodating only two men, both Scots. A further 22 navvies boarded in nearby lodging houses.

In each hut one navvy was designated "boarding house keeper". Invariably he was accompanied by his wife and, occasionally, children. The wife, presumably, attended to the domestic arrangements of the hut. None of the other occupants were accompanied by their families. In addition to railway labourers, the Moorcock huts accommodated two blacksmiths, four stone masons, two wood sawyers and one engine driver, all connected with the railway construction. A railway sub-contractor employing six men, an inspector of railway works and a master mason resided in separate lodgings nearby.

Messrs. Benton and Woodiwiss were the main contractors for this stretch of the line and, for the benefit of their employees, constructed a reading room at their depot. *The Bedale and Northallerton Times* reported in 1875 that "Penny Readings" were frequently arranged at the reading room to provide the navvies with:

a recreation of an educational tendency that would improve and develop their mental and moral powers ... and would also have an affect of counteracting the evil influences arising from the social plague spots – public houses.

The reporter does not say how many navvies attended the "Penny Readings" in preference to the public house!

Contrary to the generally accepted view that most navvies were from Ireland, the Moorcock navvies came from all parts of the British Isles.

Many navvies travelled the country to find work wherever railway construction was taking place. This mobility of the navvy can be plotted by studying the birthplaces of his dependants.

An impression of the numbers of navvies employed in Wensleydale can be gained by a projection based on the 164 workers employed in constructing the six miles of the Midland branch. If it is assumed that the labour employed was in direct proportion to the length of the line, approximately 600 workers may have been employed on railway construction in Wensleydale in the mid 1870s.

It is possible from these numbers and knowing the national average wages paid to navvies, to estimate that the total annual wages bill paid to Wensleydale navvies would be in the order of £38,500. Some of the navvies' wages will have been saved to send to relatives living out of the dale, but it is likely that at least one third, or about £12,800, was spent in Wensleydale. The dale's community will also have been helped by locals, possibly numbering about one hundred, who worked as navvies. They and their families will have enjoyed a reasonable standard of living with a steady and relatively high wage coming into the household during the building of the railway.

Some local people took advantage of the demand for

Birthplace of Moorcock navvies 1871

Wensleydale	23
Yorkshire	4
Northern	11
North West	15
West Midlands	8
East Midlands	4
East Anglia	8
South West	12
South East	24
Wales	3
Scotland	9
Ireland	14
Not Known	7
Total	142

For convenience, the classification used is based on the present day Economic Planning Regions

Birthplaces of one navvy and his family resident at the Moorcock Settlement, 1871

Person	Birthplace
Railway Labourer/ Hut keeper	Berkshire
Wife	Ireland
Child – 7 years	Essex
Child – 4 years	Middlesex (Holloway)
Child – 3 years	Middlesex (Hendon)
Child – 1 year	Leicester

their goods by railway employees during the period of construction. Milk, particularly, was in great demand and was sold at an inflated price. This was regarded as an acceptable practice during the construction but in 1879, after the completion of the line, there was an outcry at the continuation of the high prices which were causing distress to the poor in the locality. The Earl of Wharncliffe, in retaliation to the monopoly of the milk traders, established a milk herd and proceeded to sell milk at the old rate. In the face of this competition the other milk sellers were forced to lower their prices.

The impact of this influx of navvies on the local population was, therefore, not always positive. Fears regarding the impending invasion had been growing since the first proposals had been advanced in the 1840s and the navvies in the 1870s were certainly not averse to fighting. For example, in July 1878 the usual large contingent of Irishmen arrived in Hawes for the annual hirings for haytime work. Unfortunately, it was not a good year and many failed to obtain employment. Quarrelling broke out which soon developed into a running street battle between the Irish and the railway navvies and it was some time before the situation was brought under control.

As construction of the line drew nearer completion, local interest heightened with the hopes of increased trade and prosperity for the area. However, the dale did not enjoy complete harmony and some inter-settlement rivalry erupted in the form of a heated exchange between the residents of Askrigg and Hawes which appeared in *The Bedale and Northallerton Times* in 1876-77.

Askrigg had been in decline as a market town since the early nineteenth century when the rapid expansion of Hawes, due partly to the re-routing of the turnpike road, led to its usurping Askrigg's position as the main centre of the upper dale. Askrigg's fortunes had declined so rapidly that even its once thriving market had been abandoned in the 1850s. However, with the prospect of the railway the villagers of Askrigg had successfully revived the market in the mid 1870s, had improved facilities in the village and intended to build a large market hall. These activities were noted by John Routh, a resident of Hawes, with the following comment:

A gigantic farce is being enacted weekly at the antiquated old relic of barbarism known as Askrigg; the performance being nothing less than an attempt to revive that long ago defunct and recently buried nonentity called Askrigg market.

He stated that he had visited Askrigg on market day in search of the market but without success. In his concluding comments Routh hurled a final insult by suggesting that the village name was derived from "Ass-Rigg" – the first inhabitant being an ass whose skeleton was discovered under a mound or "rigg"!

As can be imagined, this outrageous article brought a speedy response from Askrigg. The tone of the reply was moderate, stating that there was enough potential for both places to expand their trade with the arrival of the railway. The writer, Stockdale Thompson, further commented that on the day of Routh's visit there had been no fewer than 700 sheep for sale. In addition pigs and poultry were plentiful and 31 tradesmen with various goods and more than 20 baskets of butter met with a ready sale. The correspondent concluded drily that it must

The settlement for railway workers in the bleak countryside at Garsdale Head, 1977. (G.E. Hallas)

taken a donkey from Hawes to write such untruths! Unfortunately, Askrigg's valiant attempts to revive its fortunes failed and the market declined. Only 40 head of cattle were offered at the November Fair in 1878 so the market was finally abandoned.

4 Opening of the line

The N.E.R. line between Leyburn and Hawes was completed by the end of 1876. On the first inspection the Board of Trade official discovered several deficiencies that required rectifying. These were quickly attended to and following the next visit the inspector recommended that the Board of Trade sanction the opening of the line on condition that certain station services at Aysgarth and Leyburn were completed.

So after 30 years of patient waiting by the people of Wensleydale the line was opened between Leyburn and Askrigg on 1 February 1877. The remaining stretch to Hawes could not be opened until the Midland Railway Company completed construction of the joint station at

Mossdale Head tunnel between Hawes and Garsdale. (J W Armstrong)

Hawes. This work took another year. The date for the complete opening of the N.E.R. Leyburn to Hawes line was to be 1 May 1878 but further delays occurred and the line was eventually opened for goods and passengers on 1 June 1878.

When the Bedale and Leyburn Railway had opened some 20 years earlier, the occasion had been celebrated at the new stations with public dinners, music and fireworks and the opening of the Leyburn-Askrigg section in 1877 followed the same tradition. Flags were hung, triumphal arches spanned the streets, church bells were rung and crowds, many in fancy dress, gathered at each station to welcome the first train into the dale. When the train arrived at Askrigg at 9.20 a.m. it was greeted by a brass band from Swaledale. A village tea was provided and many residents travelled on the return train which departed at 5 p.m. Due to the overwhelming demand for places an extra train was provided which departed at 8 p.m. when a firework display concluded the celebrations.

The arrival of the railway was not welcomed unreservedly. One local person commented that he had been able to live in Wensleydale for 70 years without railways and "such like foolery" and, therefore, should be allowed to live his "bit of time" out quietly without commotion.

Nevertheless, many people quickly took advantage of the new service between Leyburn and Askrigg. In July 1877 a total of 3,197 tickets were sold at the four new stations of Wensley, Redmire, Aysgarth, and Askrigg and in June 1878, 906 N.E.R. tickets were purchased at the new Hawes terminus.

As early as 1876 work on the short Midland branch was behind schedule. This was partly due to the difficult terrain. Some sections of the line were being constantly undermined and the tunnel construction was causing continual problems, and in 1876 several embankments and cuttings still awaited construction. The delays led to an escalation in costs of the six-mile branch line.

The Midland branch between Hawes and Hawes Junction was due to be opened in July 1878 but further problems arose and the opening date was postponed. The Board of Trade inspector passed the line for freight and the line opened for goods traffic on 1 August. The inspector and Midland officials travelled on the line on 6 August when it was declared safe for passenger traffic. The passenger service was to commence on Saturday, 10 August but was postponed when the N.E.R. and Midland Company failed to agree working arrangements. The problems were not resolved until late September and the branch finally opened to passengers on Tuesday, 1 October 1878. Initially the Midland Company agreed to pay the N.E.R. £500 per annum to run all trains between Hawes and Hawes Junction but early in the twentieth century the Midland ran some of their own stock over the branch.

The new six-mile line was hailed as extremely picturesque, especially where, after leaving the gloom of Mossdale tunnel, Mossdale Gill Falls offered a breath-taking sight.

One private passenger train travelled the 20-minute

Engine No 588 at Leyburn station. The engine was built at Gateshead in 1877 and opened the last section of the Wensleydale Railway. (K.A. Bell collection)

31

Old Faithful No 67345 pulls into Askrigg station – the scene of much jubilation in 1877 following the line's long-awaited opening. (N.E. Stead collection)

journey on the new branch line before it was officially opened to passengers. Lord and Lady Wharncliffe were visiting their shooting box at Simonstone near Hawes and were conveyed the short distance by special train in a Midland saloon carriage. Their arrival at Hawes station was greeted with lively music played by the local brass band.

When the first regular passenger train passed over the line on the opening day it carried a number of N.E.R. officials in addition to the many eager members of the public. The 10.37 a.m. Midland train from Carlisle was scheduled to connect with the new branch service at Hawes Junction but, due to delays caused further north by extra traffic travelling to Brough Hill Fair, the connection on this first day was missed. Although the new service was usually efficient, the problems encountered on 1 October served to remind intending rail users that on occasions difficulties would arise.

So by the end of 1878 Wensleydale at last enjoyed a through connection giving access to both west and east railway systems and the opportunity for dales people to travel with comparative ease the length and breadth of the country.

The engines that served the community were held in high regard locally and some were given special names. The one that pulled the afternoon passenger train between Hawes Junction and Hawes was known affectionately as "Boniface" and the GS engine No 67345 that served the

dale between Leyburn and Hawes was designated "Old Faithful".

Railway personnel

The railway staff were generally not from the Wensleydale area and did not fit naturally into the hierarchy of rural life. Their relatively high wages in the 1870s made them the aristocracy of labour and the station master was usually a much respected, though somewhat isolated, member of the community he served.

The number of railway employees in the dale was never great. In 1861, five years after the opening of the Leyburn terminus, only eight people were employed by the N.E.R. Their jobs were as follows: one engine driver, two locomotive firemen, one station master, one clerk and three porters. However, by 1869 the numbers had increased and, apart from other workers, eight staff were employed at the station office with an annual station

	1870				1890				1910				1929			
	Staff	£	s	d	Staff	£	s	d	Staff	£	s	d	Staff	£	s	d
Station Master	1	78	0	0	1	78	0	0	1	125	0	0[1]	1	286	7	4
Clerks (passenger)	2	34	0	0	1	65	0	0	2	53	2	9	2	200	5	10
Clerks (goods)	1	10	8	0	2	35	0	0	3	49	9	4	2	233	4	10
Clerks (minerals)	-		-		1	35	0	0	1	46	11	6	1	48	10	8
Porters (passenger)	2	45	10	0	3	47	13	4	4	52	0	0	5	101	19	11
Porters (goods)	1	44	4	0	2	39	0	0	2	37	0	3	1	108	9	1
Guards	1	54	12	0	3	63	6	8	4	77	0	0	-		-	
Signalmen	-		-		2	61	2	0	2	56	10	9	3	139	8	4
Pensioner (ex-porter)	-		-		1	19	10	0	-		-		-		-	
Total staff and wages	8	346	4	0	16	800	14	0	19	1129	7	0	15	22238	13	0

[1] Salary for 1909

top: Askrigg station staff circa 1909. (R. Hugill collection)

above: Redmire platelayers' gang near Jervaulx station. (Mrs E. Peacock collection)

right: Aysgarth station staff circa 1900. (J. Dinsdale collection)

wages bill of £341 6s. Three years later a total of sixteen (eight station staff and eight other workers) were based at Leyburn. The station master naturally received the highest salary. The first master, Robert Horn, was appointed in 1855 at an annual salary of approximately £80 and a rent free house. This salary was later stabilised at £78 and remained at the same level for many years. The numbers employed at Leyburn station office continued to rise to a maximum of nineteen at the turn of the century, when the annual wages bill was about £1,000. The table of salaries shows staff numbers and wages per person at Leyburn between 1870 and 1929 and illustrates the changing structure of the station staff and movements of wages which did not automatically rise annually. The apparent inconsistencies in some of the wages paid may be explained by variations in hours worked.

Leyburn station staff and wages 1870 -1929

The 1881 census, taken three years after the opening of the whole line returned 65 men employed on the Wensleydale railway. In addition to fourteen based at Leyburn, eight were based at Wensley, five at Redmire, eight at Aysgarth, nine at Askrigg and 21 at Hawes. Two signalmen, one N.E.R. employee at Wensley and one Midland employee at Hawes returned the dual occupation of Methodist local preacher. One employee at Askrigg was a locomotive cleaner. Several workers lived in railway cottages along the line and at the turn of the century were paying a weekly rent of 3s.3d. Others lived in nearby villages.

above: Leyburn station staff circa 1906

below: Hawes station staff early 20th century

The total wages for railway workers in Wensleydale in 1881 is estimated to be about £3,200 and for the first time people were employed within the dale who were paid wages geared to regional and national rather than local levels. Compared with the local agricultural workers, the wages of railway workers had the advantage of being higher and more regular.

The railway personnel worked long hours (twelve hours per day in the early twentieth century) under strict

Askrigg station staff circa 1925: Back row – Arthur Henderson (signalman), Jo Foster (porter), Bill Hugill (signalman). Front row – T. Groves (station master), Ted Wilson (clerk). (R. Hugill collection)

conditions but were generally proud to be members of their railway company. To ensure security after retirement many staff joined the N.E.R. Servants Pension Society when it was established in 1907. During the First World War many N.E.R. employees, including some working the Wensleydale line, volunteered for service in the 32nd (Reserve) Battalion, Northumberland Fusiliers (N.E.R. Pioneers).

In order to be of maximum service to the local community the railway stations were open for long hours as the following table for Leyburn demonstrates.

Leyburn station opening times							
Station to Public				Office			
Passenger		Goods		Passenger		Goods	
From	To	From	To	From	To	From	To
a.m.	p.m.	a.m.	p.m.	a.m.	p.m.	a.m.	p.m.
1907 5.45	10.30	7.0	5.0	5.45	7.30	7.30	7.0
1929 6.55	8.30	8.0	5.0	7.30	8.30	8.0	5.0

5 Architecture of the line

The domestic architecture of Wensleydale reflects the relative inaccessibility of the area before the 1870s. The traditional dales' house developed in response to a hard climate and an abundance of good local building materials. The houses almost invariably faced south, irrespective of terrain, thereby benefiting from the most favourable aspect of sunlight. Windows were rarely placed in the north elevation and were also infrequent in the west elevation, the direction of the prevailing rain-bearing winds. The buildings were generally without ornamentation and had thick stone walls to provide insulation from the weather. Roofs were gently pitched (about 30 degrees) and stone slated.

The arrival of the railway in the 1870s introduced the first major external influence on the dale's architecture. Not only were alien architectural forms imprinted on the local landscape, in the shape of railway buildings, but the railway facilitated, for the first time, the importation of non-traditional building materials, such as foreign building stone, bricks and Welsh blue slates.

The railway station buildings in Wensleydale, even today, after a century of acclimatisation, are conspicuous for their alien form. Three of the branch line stations, Leyburn (Bedale and Leyburn Railway), Wensley (N.E.R.) and Hawes (Midland) are situated on the south side of the

Hawes station earlier this century. The station is typical of the Midland Derby Gothic style. (Author's collection)

above: Wensley station in the early 1920s (K.A. Bell)

right: Wensley station in 1970s with waiting-room canopy removed. Note additional private entrance onto the platform for Lord Bolton and his family. (Mason Scarr)

line, the other three (all N.E.R.) are on the north side. The stations together with the pairs of railway workers' cottages found at intervals along the line, were built as construction of the track progressed.

The siting of the railway station took no account of prevailing weather conditions but was dictated solely by the direction of the line and proximity to the local community which the stations were to serve. Fortunately, as the railway was built on a west-east alignment the gable ends of the buildings took the brunt of the prevailing weather.

By the mid 1860s the major railway companies were beginning to standardise their stations and their designs increasingly made little concession to local circumstances. The N.E.R. and Midland companies were no exception to the general trend. The North Eastern chose the free Renaissance villa style and the Midland adopted a mock Gothic for their standard designs. Both styles were becoming increasingly popular in late Victorian England.

The four stations built by the N.E.R. on the Wensleydale line were a more rustic (cottage orné) version of the substantial villa style and could have been transplanted from almost any Victorian middle class suburb. The N.E.R., like the Midland, built to impress its customers and the small stations, with the station master's house an integral part of the design, were quietly impressive. The station master's house was a two storey building with gables to the front and rear and one of the end elevations. A flat roofed single storey services extension was attached to this end elevation. A pitched roof, single storey station office area was attached to the other end elevation. Apart from the bay window to the station office, which had the functional role of enabling the station master to observe train arrivals and departures, all the windows were of a simple four-pane sash design. Even though all the gables terminated in decorated bargeboards there was generally an absence of unnecessary ornamentation in contrast to the Midland design displayed at Hawes.

The coursed, pitch-faced sandstone used in the construction of the N.E.R. buildings was not local to upper Wensleydale and was brought into the dale, possibly from other areas where the N.E.R. was working. Welsh blue slates were used for all the station roofs. These slates had a number of economic advantages over local stone slates. Despite being imported they were cheaper, they did not require the massive roof timbers which were necessary for the heavy local slates, they came in standard sizes and, for the outside contractors who were unfamiliar with local stone slates, they were much easier to lay. However, these imported slates were less suited to resisting the effects of the hard dales' climate. A local firm, Thomas Weatherald of Askrigg, held the contract for maintenance of the station buildings and in severe weather was often called upon to refit the slates.

Aysgarth station 1977. This picture typifies the N.E.R.'s station design – a cottage orné version of the Renaissance villa style. (G.E. Hallas)

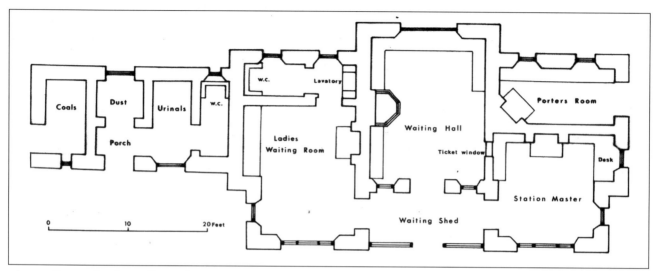

above: Hawes Station – floor plan.

below: Aysgarth station – ground floor plan.

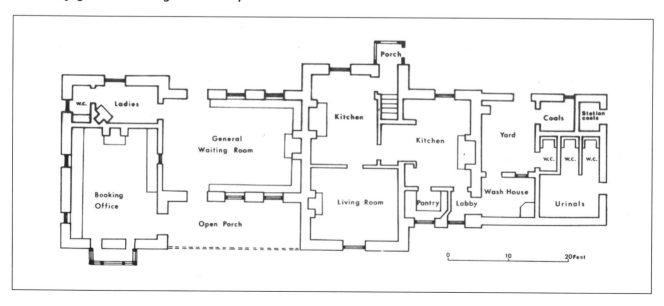

Accommodation in the station master's house comprised a living room and kitchen on the ground floor with an outer kitchen, pantry and water closet in the services extension. Four bedrooms were situated on the first floor, two of which were very small. The house had no bathroom.

The N.E.R. station design was functionally quite successful in terms of access and circulation. The approach road gave direct access to the main entrance which was set at the rear of the building. This main entrance led directly into the general waiting room from which a ticket window connected to the booking office. A second main door from the general waiting room gave access to the platform through a small porched area. The ladies room was reached direct from the general waiting room.

Although all four stations were built to the same standard design all were subject to some modification. One station, Askrigg, is the complete mirror image of the other three. Its house is attached to the west wall of the main station building. Wensley, being built south of the line, also has the house to the west of the station building. The houses at Askrigg and Wensley, therefore, receive the brunt of the prevailing winds.

It is interesting that the former Aysgarth station master has emphasised how comfortable, well-built and draught-free his station house had been whereas the widow of the former Askrigg station master has remarked how inconvenient and draughty her station house was with its back door set into the west wall.

Wensley was the only station with a significant modification. The station was built on land leased from Lord Bolton and the station area was altered to include a private waiting room, toilet and separate entrance on to the platform for the exclusive use of the Bolton family. The inclusion of this additional area was achieved by adding an extra seven feet to the overall length of the station and by reducing the size of the general waiting room.

Wensley and Aysgarth were also supplied with small waiting shelters on the opposite platform from the main station.

In the 1870s the N.E.R. buildings were progressive in both design and amenities. However, by 1954, when passenger service was withdrawn, the station houses had fallen sadly behind the majority of local houses in the amenities they enjoyed. Some of the stations had electricity, mains water and mains sewerage by 1954 but had received these considerably later than the communities they served. The more isolated stations were never connected to these services. None of the stations had electricity until the 1950s and then at some, as in the case of Askrigg, it was only supplied to the station master's house, while the platform office continued to be lit by oil. By contrast, Askrigg village had enjoyed locally generated electricity since 1908 although it was not connected to the National Grid until the 1950s. The same was true of mains water supply which most stations did not receive until the late 1940s and early 1950s. The station master's house at Wensley was connected to mains water only in 1969 after the closure of the station and Redmire station master's house was served by a pumped spring supply until the 1980s.

The Midland Railway adopted a very distinctive architectural style in its "Derby Gothic" (Derby was the headquarters of the Midland Company). The station at Hawes closely followed the standard Gothic small station design of the Company. In this plan the station master's house was not an integral part of the design and at Hawes was situated some distance away to the south west of the main platform building.

The station design had an imposing front elevation which, at Hawes, unfortunately, faced north and was very exposed. It comprised twin gables separated by a central

41

porch (described as the "waiting shed"). The main entrance was via double, panelled, wooden doors set in an elaborate screen of cast iron latticework and glass. Above each of the windows in the front elevation an attractive quatrefoil motif was set in a single dressed stone. In addition, a station clock was placed on the right-hand gable and the gables were surmounted by decorated barge-boards. The rear elevation at Hawes faced south and had a central gable of identical design to the twin gables on the north side. The end elevations were undistinguished and on the east side a low extension housed toilets and store rooms.

Hawes station was constructed in coursed, pitch faced local sandstone with dressed stone plinth, quoin, lintels and window surrounds. The steeply pitched roof (over 50 degrees) was of Welsh blue slate with decorated ridge tiles and was surmounted by two large dressed stone chimneys.

The arrangement of the rooms and access was a weak point in the overall design. The only public entrance was situated at the front of the building facing the line so intending passengers had to walk round the building to gain access. This entrance led, via the waiting shed, to the main rooms which, according to the master design should have been as follows: the central waiting hall, the ladies waiting room and water closet to the left, and the station master's room to the right. This plan was modified, possibly by N.E.R. employees who manned the station and found the original design impracticable. The waiting hall was converted to a general office which was divided by a timber screen to create a separate cubicle for the ticket clerk. The station master's room

Quatrefoil motif used at Hawes station. (G.E. Hallas)

Lampholder at Aysgarth station demonstrates the Victorian love for detail. (G.E. Hallas)

was used as a combined booking and waiting room; the ladies waiting room remained unchanged.

It was a characteristic feature of the Midland stations that the main building was carefully balanced by a smaller platform shelter building on the opposite side of the line and Hawes station was no exception. The platform shelter had a simple rectangular design with most of the internal space occupied by a main waiting room. A toilet was situated at the west end. The overall design of windows, stonework, bargeboards and motifs (trefoil this time) complemented those of the main building.

Although the Hawes Junction buildings at Garsdale were strictly on the Settle-Carlisle line they were effectively the terminus for the Wensleydale line. Hawes Junction served no particular local community and functioned simply as an "exchange" so no main station building was constructed. Its junction role was served simply by the use of modified platform shelters on both sides of the line. These, in contrast to the usual Midland platform shelter, were equipped with fireplaces. The main shelter on the central platform had an elaborate glass and iron canopy which was removed in 1957 when renovations were undertaken.

At one time the waiting room was used to hold church services (as was the one at Hawes). It also housed a library of some two hundred books donated by two sisters who had, on one occasion, been stranded for some time at the station. The library was available for the use of passengers and railway employees. A room was also provided under the nearby water tank for social gatherings. Hawes Junction with its row of railway cottages was a focus of life on this remote watershed.

The two-storey building at Leyburn constructed by the Bedale and Leyburn Railway Company did not follow a standard design. The station master's house was an integral part of the design and, in addition, there was a large separate first floor room which served as a boardroom for the Bedale and Leyburn directors. Passengers gained access to the platform through an archway in which was situated the booking hall with a ticket window and an entrance to the waiting room.

Station accommodation at Leyburn initially comprised a booking office, goods office, general waiting room and

Engine shed, water tower and turntable at Leyburn station (1964), now all demolished. (J W Armstrong)

Askrigg station circa 1909 – the mirror image of other N.E.R.. Wensleydale stations. Note the station master, Mr Thorpe, in his frock coat. (R. Hugill collection)

ladies first class waiting room. In the 1870s the accommodation was expanded to include a lamp room, coal office and gentlemen's first class waiting room, and in 1893 a separate office was provided for the station master. In 1876 an up platform of 317 feet was constructed which, along with the original down platform, was extended in the 1880s. In 1885 a waiting shed with a stove was supplied on the up platform and an iron footbridge spanned the line to connect the two platforms.

The station yards on the Wensleydale line provided vital support services for the railway. Four of the stations,

Leyburn, Aysgarth, Askrigg and Hawes had goods warehouses which enabled freight to be loaded and unloaded from trucks and stored while awaiting collection or dispatch. The buildings are generally plain in design but the massive warehouse (built 1883) at Hawes reflected the Derby Gothic in its overall style. Not all the stations were served by two platforms, Redmire and Askrigg each had only one. Unusually the up platform at Wensley was staggered and was sited some distance to the east of the main platform, beyond the nearby level crossing. The platforms at Leyburn were also slightly staggered.

A good example of Midland "Derby Gothic". Dent Station on the Settle-Carlisle line, 1977. (G.E. Hallas)

All the stations included at least one signal cabin and a coal depot containing several cells (Leyburn had ten separate holding cells). Some stations followed Leyburn in having a horse and cattle loading dock, a carriage loading platform and livestock enclosures.

Leyburn was also supplied with a turntable, water columns and a locomotive shed as was Hawes Junction. Several stations had cranes and all were equipped with Pooley weighing machines. Askrigg was supplied with four, including a cart weighbridge for the goods yard (supplied 1873); a goods warehouse platform machine (1875); and a counter machine for the parcels office (1878). Aysgarth also had four machines and Leyburn was equipped with five. In both these places not all the original models survived the life of the line. The three machines at Redmire and the two at Wensley were original models and were in use up to the final closure in the 1960s. All the stations included at least one cart weighbridge and at Leyburn station the Keld Heads (lead) mining Company, which had its own coal depot, had installed an additional weighing machine.

6 Operation of the line: passenger traffic

Local traffic

The completed line in Wensleydale was opened to passengers on 1 October 1878 and immediately dales people explored the potential offered by the railway. The new service provided easy access to neighbouring villages and also the opportunity to travel in reasonable comfort and speed to all parts of the country.

The Leyburn terminus had issued nearly 14,000 passenger tickets per annum as early as 1868 and the annual figure increased rapidly to a peak of 26,000 in 1880 when the new line opened. Thereafter, the number of passenger tickets issued at Leyburn remained stable but rose immediately after the First World War and in 1919 over 38,500 tickets were sold. After this date there began an unremitting decline which was gradual in the 1920s but rapidly gained momentum in the 1930s until in 1938 only 5,000 passenger tickets were issued.

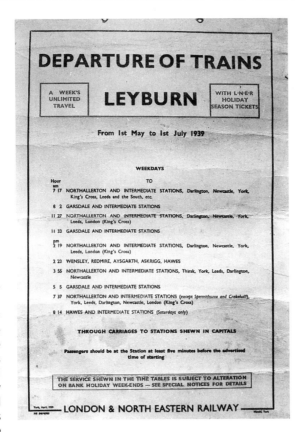

Departures from Leyburn station, 1939.
(R. Tyson collection)

The combined total of passenger tickets for the six N.E.R. stations (including Leyburn) demonstrates a similar dramatic increase and subsequent decline. In 1878, despite the fact that the N.E.R. line had been operating to Hawes for only seven months, a total of 74,000 tickets were issued. Two years later, as the dales people made greater use of the services offered by the railway, over 85,000 tickets were issued. This was followed by a slight decline which stabilised at an average of about 75,000 tickets per annum until the turn of the century. From 1905 there was a significant rise and in 1910 over 83,000 tickets were sold. Although, there was a decline in passenger travel during the First World War, post-war passenger traffic recovered and reached a peak of over 89,000 tickets in the early 1920s. However, during the inter-war period motor transport increased in popularity and there was a progressive decline in rail travel. By 1930 only 30,000 tickets were issued at the six N.E.R. stations and by 1935 this figure had fallen by a further 40 per cent to 18,000. The decline, although varying in severity, continued unabated until the closure of passenger services in April 1954.

No 41304 crossing Appersett Viaduct heading for Garsdale. (N.E.Stead Collection)

The Midland branch between Hawes and Hawes Junction never carried substantial passenger traffic. In 1879, the first full year of operation, 6,845 tickets were purchased. This figure rose to over 8,000 the following year and for the next 40 years passenger figures fluctuated between 7,000 and 9,000 with a peak of 9,193 tickets being issued in 1891. In the late 1920s, following the same trend as that of the N.E.R. stations, passenger traffic declined steadily until March 1959 when the passenger service between Hawes and Hawes Junction finally closed.

Although motor transport dealt the final blow to the Wensleydale line it was not the sole cause of the line's demise. Wensleydale and Swaledale had been suffering from a declining population for many years. The population of Wensleydale had reached a peak of 8,648 in 1861 but by 1901 the dale had lost nearly one quarter of that population. Upper Swaledale (whose people used the Wensleydale line) had suffered even greater losses and by 1901 its population had fallen by two-thirds from its 1821 peak of 7,480.

Local people had hoped that the new railway would arrest the decline but as the below table graphically demonstrates, the hope was not realised and the population continued to fall.

For those who remained in the dales the railway in the nineteenth and early twentieth century became a lifeline. Not only was rail transport used for social and business visits but markets near and far afield could be attended. The people of upper Swaledale travelled over one of three moorland passes to catch the train at either Hawes, Askrigg or Redmire. The Buttertubs Pass and the Askrigg to Swaledale road traversed high ground of over 1,700 feet above sea level, and for long periods during winter drifting snow frequently severed connections between the two dales. Despite these problems the Swaledale farmers made regular use of the railway.

The diary of one such nineteenth century yeoman farmer demonstrates the importance of the railway for local people. Before the line was opened in upper Wensleydale, Swaledale people travelled to the nearest station either at Richmond (opened 1846) or Leyburn. In 1851, the diarist, Francis Garth, notes "At Richmond … and went forward to the Great Exhibition of the Industry of All Nations held at Hyde Park". He saw the most recent farm machinery at the exhibition and gained information on the latest farming techniques, some of which he was able to put into practice.

Garth noted the opening of the Wensleydale line to Askrigg in February 1877 and on 5 March took his first

Population of Wensleydale and Upper Swaledale

	Upper Wensleydale[1]	Lower Wensleydale[2]	Wensleydale	Upper Swaledale[3]
1851	5,635	2,655	8,290	6,820
1901	4,508	1,998	6,506	2,520
1951	3,607	2,370	5,977	2,088

[1]. Aysgarth westwards   [2]. Leyburn westwards   [3]. Marrick westwards

railway journey from Askrigg to visit Darlington market. Later the same year he journeyed further, boarding the train at Askrigg and travelling via Northallerton to London where he spent a few days. He then proceeded to Dorset for a short stay and finally on to Manchester for two days before returning home. The Midland branch to Hawes was not opened so he had to return via Northallerton to Askrigg.

After the complete line was opened to passengers the Garth family travelled extensively to agricultural shows and markets, visited London regularly and took holidays at the popular Victorian holiday resorts at Harrogate, Scarborough, Bridlington and Lytham St Anne's. In the early twentieth century, Francis Garth's daughter continued the diary. Several of her comments presage the end of the railway. In 1900 the winter coal was brought to the farm by traction engine, in 1907 she purchased a bicycle and in 1912 she recorded her first car drive in a four-seater Rover. The era of motor transport was being ushered in.

In addition to adult passengers, the railway played a vital role in the education of some of the dale's children. In the early twentieth century scholarship children were able to travel daily to Northallerton Grammar School, a journey of up to 40 miles. Normally the children arrived at Northallerton by 8.30 a.m. but occasionally the train was late. The cause of the delay was usually a long halt at Wensley station where, when Lord Bolton or members of his family wished to travel, the train was instructed to await the arrival of the aristocratic party. Because of this extenuating circumstance the children were excused punishment for late arrival at school. After 1932, when Yorebridge Grammar School was re-housed in a fine new building at Askrigg, children from other parts of the dale travelled to the school by rail. Most pupils returned home each day but some, from the more remote areas boarded in the village.

Frequently special excursion trains enabled people from Wensleydale to visit the seaside and other places of interest. As early as 1856 a special train was laid on to take people from Leyburn to Newcastle races. In 1881 an excursion ran from the dale to Edinburgh and Glasgow. And in the summer of 1923, for example, there were six excursions from Wensleydale, one to York and Scarborough, one to Newcastle, one to Leeds and three to Saltburn.

The line, therefore, opened up new and exciting opportunities for travel to many destinations for dales people from all walks of life whether they were aristocrats or school children, farmers or holidaying families.

The first passenger service timetable for the N.E.R. line between Leyburn and Hawes was published in July 1978. Initially there were three return trains daily all connecting with Northallerton and intermediate stations as the table shows.

Wensleydale line passenger traffic, 1878

		a.m.	a.m.	p.m.
Northallerton	dep.	7.40	10.41	3.55
Leyburn	arr.	8.35	11.40	5.00
Leyburn	dep.	8.40	11.45	5.50
Wensley		8.47	11.52	5.57
Redmire		8.54	11.59	6.04
Aysgarth		9.03	12.08	6.13
Askrigg		9.15	12.20	6.25
Hawes		9.25	12.30	6.35
		a.m.	a.m.	p.m.
Hawes	dep.	7.50	10.55	4.50
Askrigg		8.00	11.05	5.00
Aysgarth		8.12	11.17	5.12
Redmire		8.21	11.26	5.21
Wensley		8.28	11.33	5.28
Leyburn	arr.	8.35	11.40	5.35
Leyburn	dep.	8.40	11.45	6.00
Northallerton	arr.	9.40	12.45	7.00

Passenger train arrives at Hawes. (N.E. Stead collection)

A new timetable was published in September 1878 in anticipation of the opening of the short Midland section. All existing passenger trains were run on to Hawes Junction and there were two additional daily trains, one from Hawes Junction to Leyburn departing at 6.15 p.m. and the other form Leyburn to Hawes departing at 2.45 p.m. (from July 1880 this train was run on to Hawes Junction). Two months later an extra train was run from Hawes Junction to Leyburn departing at 1.20 p.m. and the following year an evening train was run between Leyburn and Hawes departing at 7.40 p.m.

Wensleydale line passenger traffic, weekdays c. 1904

		a.m.	a.m.	p.m.	p.m.	p.m.	p.m.
Northallerton	dep.	7.35	10.50	1.35	3.55	6.30	9.40
Leyburn	arr.	8.32	11.39	2.30	4.52	7.20	10.30
Leyburn	dep.	8.38	11.44	2.37	4.59	7.30	-
Wensley		8.44	11.49	2.43	5.05	7.36	-
Redmire		8.49	11.54	2.48	5.10	7.41	-
Aysgarth		8.56	12.01	2.56	5.17	7.49	-
Askrigg		9.06	12.11	3.05	5.27	7.59	-
Hawes	arr.	9.15	12.20	3.14	5.36	8.08	-
Hawes	dep.	10.10	12.22	-	5.37	8.10	-
Hawes Jctn.	arr.	10.25	12.36	-	5.52	8.25	-

		a.m.	a.m.	p.m.	p.m.	p.m.	p.m.
Hawes Jctn.	dep.	-	7.10	10.50	1.05	-	6.25
Hawes		-	7.22	11.02	1.17	3.38	6.37
Askrigg		-	7.30	11.10	1.25	3.47	6.45
Aysgarth		-	7.39	11.19	1.34	3.56	6.54
Redmire		-	7.46	11.26	1.41	4.03	7.01
Wensley		-	7.51	11.30	1.46	4.08	7.06
Leyburn	arr.	-	7.56	11.35	1.51	4.13	7.11
Leyburn	dep.	6.00	7.58	11.40	1.56	4.18	7.24
Northallerton	arr.	6.50	8.45	12.30	2.45	5.05	8.12

By 1880, therefore, five return passenger trains were serving Wensleydale daily with the exception of Sundays

when the line was closed. A report in 1895 states that the daily passenger trains which ran the 39 miles 65 chain journey from Northallerton to Hawes Junction took an average load of four carriages in winter and six carriages in summer: two engines worked this traffic. The passenger service between Leyburn and Hawes of five trains daily continued almost without interruption, though with some alterations of times, until 1940 when the service was reduced to three trains per day. These departed from Leyburn at 8.08 a.m., 12.28 p.m. and 5.08 p.m. and from Hawes Junction at 10.45 a.m., 3.38 p.m. and 6.30 p.m. In the immediate post war period four trains were run daily but the service was soon curtailed and by 1954 only two return passenger trains per day served the line. During the twentieth century passenger carriages were attached to the Sunday milk train providing a skeletal service for the public.

Staff and a passenger await the arrival of the train at Aysgarth Station, 1903. (M. Kirby collection)

The dales people, even in the early days, did not always feel that they were being provided with the most efficient service. In February 1880 a petition was presented to the N.E.R. directors requesting a late evening train. The petition was unsuccessful and despite a further request the dales people were not granted a train later than the existing 7.40 p.m. from Leyburn. The following year the Rev. H. Bell lodged a complaint about the poor service from Bedale to Leyburn. The complaint was noted but apparently not acted upon.

Revenue from the passenger service was never high. Receipts from Leyburn passengers reached a nineteenth century peak of £3,684 in 1874 and thereafter dipped slightly and remained at about £2,800 per annum until 1918 when there was a sharp rise to £5,829. Revenue from passenger receipts at Leyburn began to fall in the 1920s and by 1939 was only £1,894 per annum.

Returns available for passenger traffic for all six N.E.R. stations include receipts for parcels, horses, carriages and dogs. In 1885 this traffic on the Midland and N.E.R. lines in Wensleydale brought a combined revenue of nearly £10,000. This rose to £12,538 in 1910. Receipts continued to rise into the post-war period but thereafter followed the now predictable trend of decline until the closure of the passenger service.

Although no serious accidents occurred on the Wensleydale line rail passengers did not always enjoy an uneventful journey. Shortly after the line opened in 1878 a passenger train engine was derailed on a curve between Redmire and Carperby but there were no casualties. Disruptions to services were often caused by the vagaries of the weather. On 3 June 1908 isolated but violent storms hit parts of upper Wensleydale and caused extensive flooding. The ballast under the line at Bowbridge, west of

Worsdell A Class train passing in front of Bolton Castle between Redmire and Aysgarth early this century.
(R. Tyson collection)

Askrigg, was washed away as a passenger train approached. The train stopped but was in danger of being derailed as the flood waters rushing from the moors increased. The driver saved the train and the lives of his passengers by moving the train slowing over the bridge. As the final carriage left the bridge the flood waters swept away both sleepers and rails. The train was again brought to a standstill at Askrigg station, unable to proceed as a bridge to the east of the village had also been undermined. Passengers were eventually conveyed by wagonette via Bainbridge to Aysgarth which had been virtually unaffected by the storms.

Other minor mishaps occurred. In January 1920, a tree on the line between Aysgarth and Askrigg caused the 7.20 a.m. train from Northallerton to reverse back to Aysgarth station. The obstruction was quickly removed and the train proceeded. In May 1921 a train from Northallerton reported running over some lambs near Askrigg, on investigation it was discovered that one had its legs amputated in the accident. In November 1924 a furniture van badly damaged a rail bridge crossing the road and trains were delayed until the bridge could be made safe. And in August 1927 the 4.11 p.m. Northallerton to Hawes knocked down a cow being driven over an occupation road, the train was delayed for a mere two minutes but the animal had to be destroyed.

During bad winters trains were frequently subject to long delays and passengers had to wait, often in freezing conditions, before a relief train equipped with a snowplough arrived to rescue them.

In the twentieth century services were disrupted on several occasions by industrial disputes. In 1919 the passenger service was affected between 27 September and 6 October. Initially all railway personnel reported for duty but after two days a few men joined the strike. A milk train ran on 28 September but no other trains ran until 3 October when a skeletal service of one passenger and one goods train ran daily. A miners' strike in October 1920 caused concern about the availability of stocks to keep the engines in steam. No problem occurred until March 1921 when, due to the strike, several passenger trains were cancelled and in May some railway staff joined the strike. The strike was resolved in July after much disruption, particularly to passenger traffic.

On 4 May 1926, during the General Strike, a few Wensleydale railway personnel stopped work and services were affected causing a rail motor bus to be laid on between Northallerton and Hawes. However, the staff quickly returned to work and worked normally until the strike was settled on 12 May. The continuation of the miners' action led to a restricted service on the line.

Other difficulties were encountered by individual passengers. In July 1878 an elderly resident of Aysgarth hurried to the station to catch the 8 a.m. train to Wensley. Unfortunately, on arrival at the platform after climbing the steep hill from Aysgarth Falls he suffered a fatal heart attack. Another passenger was more fortunate. In November 1878, a woman who was in a distressed condition when she boarded the train at Hawes en route for Leyburn had given birth by the time the train reached Askrigg. Both mother and child survived the ordeal and eventually recovered sufficiently to complete their journey.

Tourists and other visitors

After the opening of the station at Leyburn the opportunities for visitors to explore Wensleydale were vastly improved. During the summer months excursion trains ran frequently to Leyburn. On 14 August 1858, two special excursions arrived, one from Newcastle bringing about 100 trippers and the other from Darlington carrying some 200 members of Mechanics' Institutes. In August 1860, 450 clerks and officials from the stations of Newcastle and South Shields arrived at Leyburn for a day's outing.

During this period, after the opening of the Leyburn terminus in 1856, several small guide books were published in anticipation of the arrival of the visitors. *Wanderings in Wensleydale* by George Hardcastle was first published in 1864. The booklet informed visitors that travel in Wensleydale beyond Leyburn was extremely difficult as "at present no public conveyance exits in Wensleydale". The intrepid traveller was advised that he must hire his own vehicle and brave poor roads in order to experience the beauties of the upper dale. Neighbouring Swaledale was considered out of reach to all but the hardiest traveller.

The booklet further commented that all the available lodgings were clean and comfortable but suffered from one serious disadvantage. The sash windows would open only at the bottom and, therefore, all the smoke above this low level remained in the room causing discomfiture when the visitor stood up. Further, many bedroom fireplaces were boarded up and this prevented the pure night air from entering the room via the chimney.

The visitor was warned to dress sensibly when venturing out and was instructed to carry a spare pair of shoes and socks. George Hardcastle further advised ladies that, as long as their "preposterous" fashion of steel-hooped petticoats prevailed, they would be unable to cope with the narrow Wensleydale styles!

For those who were prepared to risk these inconveniences and seek the beauty of the dale the booklet noted that cheap tickets were available for tourists from Newcastle and Sunderland to travel to Leyburn, departing Tyneside at 4.30 p.m. on Saturdays and returning from Leyburn at 6.50 a.m. on Monday morning for arrival at Tyneside before 10 a.m. Hardcastle, commented that this arrangement did not suit business men and their assistants and demanded a Sunday service which would enable more people to enjoy Wensleydale.

After the completion of the line in 1878 many people visited the dale. Buyers from the industrial cities of the West Riding and Lancashire attended the markets to bid for cattle and sheep to feed the rapidly expanding urban population, emigrants returned to visit families and, for the first time, substantial numbers of tourists arrived to enjoy the beauties of the upper dale.

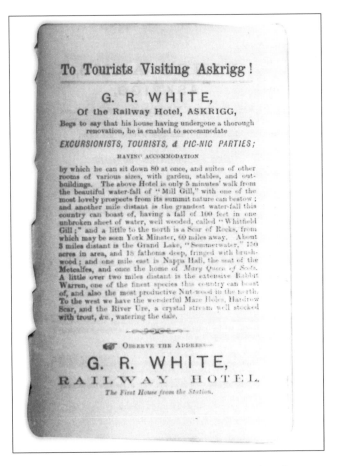

Advertisement in a tourist guide book for the short-lived Railway Hotel at Askrigg. (Author's collection)

The Midland Company immediately announced plans to provide frequent and cheap opportunities for the "operative classes" in the commercial centres of Yorkshire to travel to the dale. Advertisements appeared in the tourist guides for many small hotels and boarding houses with "well aired beds" and for the hire of conveyances to transport visitors to the local beauty spots of Hardrow Scar, Semerwater and Mill Gill Force.

In late August 1879 the Midland Company ran two cheap excursion trains to Hawes, one from Bradford arrived with 600 people and the other from Leeds carried 400 people. The main attraction for these visitors was Hardrow Scar which, in Victorian and Edwardian England was the scene of several open-air band concerts. This influx of tourists encouraged the publication of further tourist guides.

In 1884 C. Horner revised George Hardcastle's earlier work. He noted that travel in Wensleydale was greatly improved by the opening of the new railway and that journey times to Leyburn from the industrial centres were as follows:

Sunderland and Newcastle via Northallerton   3½ hours
Manchester and Liverpool via Hawes   3 hours
Leeds and Bradford (either route)   3½ hours
York via Northallerton   2½ hours

Pleasure seekers can leave Leeds by the N.E.R. and return by the Midland and vice versa throughout the summer months providing visitors with a beautiful scenic rail journey.

Horner commented that travellers should not be deterred by such obstacles as the many streams which often required wading through, the narrow stiles, or the droves of moorland cattle which were likely to survey the visitors with close, but good humoured attention. He noted also that there were excellent opportunities in

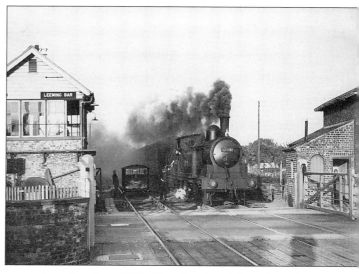

Leeming Bar, 1953. The signalman is exchanging tablets to permit the G5 No 67318 to travel in the next section of the line. (J.W.Hague/G.Ward collection)

Wensleydale for the fishing of trout and grayling.

By the 1890s the N.E.R. was advertising cheap circular tours to be run in conjunction with the Midland Railway Company. The routes and cost of the most popular rail journeys were as follows:

Newcastle, Blackhill, Bishop Auckland, Barnard Castle, Appleby, Hawes, Leyburn, Northallerton, Darlington, Durham, Newcastle
First Class: *16s.1d;*   3rd Class: *10s.1d*

York, Thirsk, Northallerton, Darlington, Barnard Castle, Kirkby Stephen, Appleby, Hawes, Leyburn, Northallerton, York
First Class:*13s 6d;*   3rd Class: *10s 1d*

Leeds, Harrogate, Ripon, Thirsk, Northallerton, Leyburn,

Postcard showing a passenger train on the N.E.R. Wensleydale line at Askrigg. (Author's collection)

Hawes, Settle, Skipton, Bradford, Leeds
First Class: 17s.6d; 3rd Class: 10s 9d

In addition other possible connections were listed in an attempt to attract visitors from as far afield as Aberdeen, Bath, Bristol, Leicester, London, Norwich, Shrewsbury and Yarmouth.

By the early twentieth century the circular tours were well established and cheap special excursion tickets were frequently available. Hawes Junction station was advertised as being 255 miles from London and could be reached by fares of 34s 6d First Class or 20s 5d Third Class.

The railway companies also advertised the opportunities for cyclists and walkers once they had arrived by train. It seems that all possible ways of attracting tourists were explored. A new golf club was opened at

Hawes within one mile of the station which offered non-members reasonable rates of 1s per day, 3s 6d per week and 10s per month. A further "spin off" of the railway tourist industry was the development of a souvenir trade with many postcards and mementos of the area being sold.

The railway was increasingly taken advantage of by holiday makers and it is estimated that immediately prior to the First World War about 70,000 visitors annually visited the dale by train. Before the arrival of the motor car, therefore, the railway enabled tourism in this part of the Yorkshire Dales to "take off". Some visitors came for the day but many would spend some money in the area purchasing food, accommodation, or souvenirs. This revenue from

tourism would have been of great help to the dale's economy particularly in periods when there was a depression in agriculture.

Occasionally unusual groups of visitors arrived by rail. In 1927 hundreds of people, wishing to view the total eclipse of the sun, travelled to Leyburn, which was on the totality line, in order to view the phenomenon at its most spectacular.

During the Second World War additional trains carried troops and military equipment to Leyburn for nearby army camps. In early September 1939 plans were published for the conveyance of evacuee children from Tyneside. The evacuation

A crowd lines the platform of Redmire station to welcome home the returning men from the Great War, circa 1918. (W. Robinson collection)

No 62064 in Leyburn station.
(J.W. Armstrong collection)

was programmed to take place over two days, with primary school children arriving on the 10 September and pre-school children and certain classes of adult arriving on the 11 September.

Askrigg and Leyburn were designated as receiving centres for evacuees from Gateshead. Askrigg was allocated a total of 325 people and Leyburn 550. These figures were later increased to 480 and 600 respectively. Evacuees were also to be sent to Swaledale via Leyburn station.

The receiving officer at Askrigg requisitioned the nearby grammar school as a reception centre where the evacuees would be given their first meal before dispersal to the surrounding villages. The children were to be allocated with accompanying adults as follows: 77+9 – Askrigg; 24+3 – Aysgarth; 111+13 – Hawes; 21+2 – Carperby; 39+5 – Hardrow; 83+10 – West Burton and Thoralby. The remaining children were allocated to isolated hamlets. The children were to live with local families and attend the nearest village school. In the event, fewer than 300 evacuees arrived at Askrigg.

In anticipation of the influx emergency rations were dispatched to Askrigg station during August and September. These consisted of large quantities of Nestle's tinned milk, sweetened and unsweetened Cadbury's and Rowntree's chocolate, corned beef from a depot in Blackburn, biscuits from South Shields and carrier bags for personal belongings.

A second wave of evacuation took place in May 1940 when Askrigg was assigned 427 children including some pupils of Gateshead Grammar School. Again fewer than the expected number arrived and a surplus of emergency rations had to be returned to the issuing depots.

On both occasions the evacuees quickly began their homeward drift, finding rural life alien to their previous crowded urban existence. However, senior pupils taking exams remained until July 1941 before returning to Tyneside. Though the evacuees were homesick many had never been better fed and for the first time enjoyed a pollution free atmosphere. Some of the young visitors developed an affection for Wensleydale and in later years returned to settle in the area.

7 Operation of the line: goods traffic

From the 1840s onwards residents and other observers had hoped that a railway in Wensleydale would revive the ailing economy of the area. In 1876 the Darlington and Stockton Times reported that Hawes, although the centre of a rich pastoral district, was considerably disadvantaged in being 16 miles distant from the nearest railway station. It was hoped that the imminent arrival of the railway would lead to the development of the agricultural and mineral potential of the upper dale.

During 1877, in anticipation of the increased trade, Hawes established a market for dairy produce and, in September 1878, following the construction of pens to accommodate 10,000 sheep, the market committee instituted a new sheep and lamb market.

The arrival of the railway brought the opportunity for the commodities of the dale to be exported quickly and easily. No longer were local people restricted to the use of heavy carts trundling slowly over poor roads, nor did they have to move their livestock on the hoof with the attendant loss of quality, nor was their quarried stone limited to the local market because of bulk and weight. Most importantly, it was no longer necessary for farmers to convert their milk to cheese and butter – now the railway could transport fresh liquid milk to city dwellers as far afield as Tyneside and London.

Not only did the railway provide the answer to the dale's export problem it was essential also for bringing vital products into the district if the dale's economy was to compete with other areas. The goods trains imported coal, provisions, fodder, building materials and mass produced articles for the eager local consumers. It is difficult to imagine the full extent of the impact that this new transport system had on the lives of the dale's people as it propelled them from their secluded backwater into the hubbub of Victorian England.

Livestock and wool traffic

In former times the lead mining industry had played an important part in the economy of the dales but, although it lingered on in Swaledale, by the 1870s it was virtually dead in Wensleydale. So, by the late nineteenth century the economy of Wensleydale was based almost solely on agriculture and neighbouring Swaledale had become increasingly dependent upon farming activities.

Although there had been some arable farming in the area this had virtually disappeared by the mid nineteenth century when increased competition from foreign imports rendered locally grown corn uneconomic. The arrival of the railway at Richmond (1846) and Leyburn (1856) undoubtedly hastened this decline and by 1878 pastoral farming predominated. The successful rearing of cattle and sheep was, therefore, vital for the survival of the dales farmer.

Most farms were small and carried only cattle and sheep. Generally the cattle comprised a small pedigree herd of dairy shorthorns and fatstock which was driven down from Scotland, purchased at local fairs and fattened on the dales farms before being sold to the industrial areas for beef. Sheep likewise were either part of the main flock, kept for their lambs and fleeces which supplied the West Riding woollen industry, or were young sheep brought from Scottish drovers solely for fattening. Before the arrival of the railway these farming activities had been constrained by the problems of transport.

A consideration of sheep traffic at Leyburn station between 1868 and 1934 demonstrates the vital role of the

Wensleydale railway in the farming activities of the area. Leyburn was the market town for the lower dale and had a substantial livestock market. Also, until 1878, it was the nearest railway link for the upper dale. In 1868 the station handled, 5,044 sheep, sending 4,392 forward and receiving 652. By 1891 sheep traffic had reached a peak of 21,509. After a slight decline the numbers recovered to reach an all time peak of 29,240 (of which nearly 22,000 were sent forward) in 1907. Thereafter the traffic fluctuated before settling into a final decline with the arrival of motor transport in the inter-war period. By 1934 only 4,547 sheep were transported by rail. The total number of sheep forwarded from the N.E.R. stations on the line in the early twentieth century varied between 37,000 and 56,000 per annum whereas numbers received by rail never rose above 6,000 in any year.

After 1878 the upper Wensleydale stations were used extensively by Swaledale farmers. One records sending forward wool annually from Askrigg. Occasionally this totalled more than 300 fleeces with a combined weight of over 120 stones. The transportation of wool was not always without problems. An Askrigg farmer underpaid for the transport of some 600 fleeces to Skipton in August 1881 and an urgent telegraph requested him to settle the account immediately. A terse telegraph was sent from Northallerton to Askrigg in September 1881:- "Wagon containing wool detached here last night without tickets, supposed to be from you. Wire where for quick".

The flocks were shorn in July but it was the months of September and October, with the important sheep fairs, that were the busiest in terms of sheep movement. In 1868, for example, of the 4,392 sheep forwarded from Leyburn, 889 were sent out in September and a further 2,084 in October. In 1906, when 37,465 sheep were forwarded on the N.E.R. section of the Wensleydale line, 13,203 were moved in September and 13,178 in October, that is over two thirds of the annual traffic in two months.

In the face of increased foreign competition, with the arrival of refrigerated ships in the late 1870s, undoubtedly the Wensleydale line aided the farmer not only to survive but, in some cases, to expand his sheep farming activities.

The new railway was equally successful in transporting cattle and the attendant produce. In the nineteenth and early twentieth centuries the dales dairy farmers were proud of their shorthorn herds, and with good reason. The large, square framed, brown and white shorthorn was a dual-purpose animal giving both a high milk yield and good beef. However, during the inter-war years the familiar black and white Friesian, with their exceptionally high milk yield, became increasingly popular, and by the 1960s, when the railway closed to goods traffic, these were the dominant cattle locally.

The arrival of the railway in Wensleydale dealt a death blow to the traditional droving trade. However, it greatly eased the movement of fatstock cattle, both to the farms and then forward to the market. In the late nineteenth century an average of 5,500 head of cattle were forwarded and 3,000 received at Leyburn per annum. This traffic peaked with an average total of 10,699 in 1891 but then declined to 6,000 per annum in the early twentieth century.

This drop reflects the decline in the number of cattle in the dale at that period which was due both to a shift from cattle fattening into dairy farming and to a more positive move into sheep farming. Thereafter the number of cattle handled at Leyburn remained stable until the 1920s when motor transport took its toll. By 1934 fewer than 2,000 cattle were being handled per annum at Leyburn station. Thereafter the decline continued though more slowly, until closure.

The six N.E.R. stations on the line handled between 7,000 and 11,000 head of cattle annually in the early twentieth century. The movement demonstrated the same seasonality as the sheep traffic. In 1906, of the 7,870 cattle

Cattle Handled at Leyburn Station, 1871 - 1921

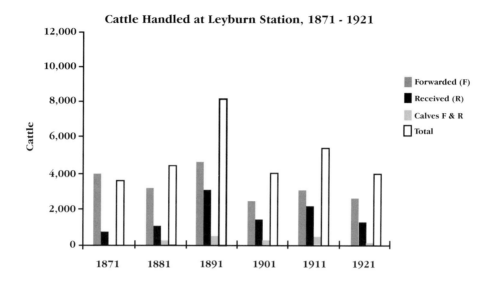

- ■ Forwarded (F)
- ■ Received (R)
- ■ Calves F & R
- □ Total

Sheep Handled at Leyburn Station, 1871 - 1921

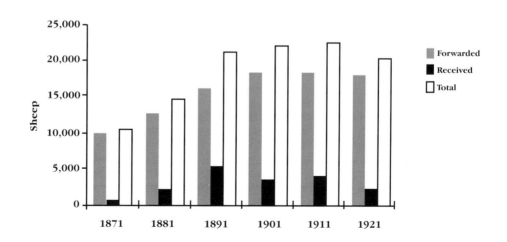

- ■ Forwarded
- ■ Received
- □ Total

handled at the N.E.R. stations in Wensleydale, 1,726 were moved in October and 2,264 in November.

Pigs and geese figured in a minor capacity in the agriculture of the dale. Most farmers reared pigs only for their own consumption and goose keeping was localised. In the early twentieth century about 650 pigs per annum were transported from Leyburn Station. After the war this traffic declined until in 1934 only 25 pigs were handled at Leyburn. Goose traffic also declined rapidly in the twentieth century and after the First World War had virtually disappeared.

The total livestock figures available for the Wensleydale line demonstrate clearly the importance of this traffic, both for the farmers and, in the late nineteenth century, for company revenue. In 1885, 37,610 head of stock were moved through the N.E.R. system and a further 10,419 were received and forwarded at Hawes over the Midland network. The traffic rapidly increased to a combined total of over 90,000 per annum in the 1890s and reached a peak of over 91,000 in 1907. Thereafter numbers fluctuated at somewhat lower levels but, by the late 1920s, an unremitting decline of livestock traffic had set in, which contributed eventually to the decision to close the line.

The scene at the stations in their hey-day presented a vastly different picture from the tranquillity generally found today. Each station held livestock in special enclosures until collected by farmers or entrained. N.E.R. regulations in the late nineteenth century allowed nine head of cattle per wagon, or 30 sheep (more if lambs) or 140 geese. Stock was not to be mixed and cattle docks and wagons were to be kept scrupulously clean. In 1881 the station at Leyburn was found to have an unclean cattle dock and the N.E.R. was fined. To ensure that the problem did not recur the company built an extra dock so that 11 cattle trucks could be loaded at any one time.

Dales people still recall clearly the hustle and bustle through the village streets as livestock was driven to and from the station. Such droving was not always without incident. On one occasion, at Askrigg, a bullock broke loose from the herd, ran through the open front door of a nearby house and up the stairs to the bedroom. Persuading the bullock to return downstairs proved more problematical.

Livestock traffic was normally handled by the one Northallerton-Hawes return goods train per day. Individuals with large numbers of stock to move ordered extra wagons to be attached to the train. On market days and autumn fair days extra trains and additional wagons were provided as a matter of course. Frequently, an early morning cattle train was run from Hawes, departing at 6.20 a.m., and carried a third class carriage to accommodate stockmen.

In November during Middleham Fair extra goods trains were sent from Stockton and Thirsk to Leyburn to take additional traffic. The Thirsk train had instructions to continue to York on the return journey if there was sufficient livestock for that destination.

Horses and dogs were also carried by rail but were usually part of the passenger traffic. The numbers were not significant other than at Leyburn station which served nearby Middleham, an important racehorse centre. In the early twentieth century about 2,000 horses per annum were handled at Leyburn. Contrary to other livestock trends this traffic expanded to reach a peak of 2,000 forwarded and 1,000 received per annum in the 1930s. From 1935, to facilitate movement of the race horses to and from the train, Leyburn station maintained a small fleet of motor horse boxes.

Milk traffic

The arrival of the railway directly influenced one major change in farming practice in Wensleydale. Prior to 1878

Milk carts and churns at Askrigg station in the early twentieth century. (M. Hartley collection)

most of the milk produced in the area was converted into butter and cheese with only a little milk retained for local consumption. But by the late nineteenth century British farmers were feeling the cold winds of competition from continental dairy produce and the Wensleydale dairy farmer desperately needed another outlet for his produce if he was to weather the economic storm. The timely arrival of a rapid transport system provided the means for survival. Now, liquid milk could be sent quickly to industrial areas and other dairy produce could play a supporting and not a dominant role. Wensleydale was not alone in this respect and many rural areas moved into large-scale liquid milk production at the time. Henry Rew in 1892 commented:

Every traveller by rail has noted the outward and visible signs of the expansion of this trade in the battalions of cans … which daily come and go along all the country lines of railway.

In the early years of the Wensleydale railway there were two systems of providing liquid milk to the cities. The first method, which had been in operation on a small scale before the 1870s, involved the keeping of cowhouses in the industrial centres, particularly Manchester and Liverpool. Often, younger members of farming families ran the businesses which were supplied with cattle sent by rail (after 1878) from the home farm in Wensleydale. When the cows ceased lactating they were exchanged with a fresh batch of cattle from Wensleydale. The businesses were generally kept within the family as a strong element of mutual trust was required. Many of the cowhouses thrived and continued into the twentieth century but, unfortunately, cattle and cities do not mix well and the cowhouses were unhygienic places. The proximity of cattle manure to both cattle and milk and the abundance of flies during the summer months frequently led to contaminated milk. Outbreaks of infectious diseases, including typhoid, diphtheria and scarlet fever, were often attributed to infected milk from the cowhouses.

The other system could only operate where there was a means of rapid transport. This involved sending the milk direct from the farm to the city consumer. The earliest reference to the movement of Wensleydale milk in this manner is in the 1890s but undoubtedly milk had been sent by rail prior to this period. In 1894 milk was sent from Wensleydale via Northallerton to Newcastle, Middlesbrough, Hull and Leeds. By 1899 milk was also being forwarded to Bradford, Halifax and other West Riding towns, and to the large milk depot at Finsbury Park for supply to London. Liverpool also received the upper dale's milk, the freight charge to farmers for this particular traffic being 1s 7d per 12 gallon Wensleydale can, and 1s 11½d per 17 gallon Wensleydale can. The total volume of milk forwarded on the N.E.R. network from Hawes, Askrigg, Aysgarth and Redmire stations was 27,000 gallons in 1899. By 1905 this traffic had risen to 426,000 gallons. The following year, when Leyburn milk traffic of 13,700 gallons was also

Farmers near Redmire return home after loading milk onto the train in January 1963 when the line had to be reopened because of snow-blocked roads. (K.A. Bell)

included, the total was in excess of 502,000 gallons. This rapid rise in milk export from the dale led to the decision to form a company which would erect a bottling depot at Northallerton to handle Wensleydale milk and forward it to Tyneside and other industrial areas.

The N.E.R. looked favourably on this scheme and an officer of the company reported during discussions:

The large towns of the country are now obtaining their milk from considerable distances away instead of from cows kept in urban and suburban districts.

Before 1899 revenue from milk traffic had been virtually non-existent on the N.E.R. network but by 1905 milk freight produced a return of £1,500 per annum. It was estimated that this revenue would rise by a further £750 if the Northallerton depot was successful and bottled all the Wensleydale milk.

The negotiations resulted in the N.E.R. agreeing to construct the bottling depot adjacent to the railway at Northallerton and to let it to the newly formed Wensleydale Pure Milk Society (W.P.M.S.) at a rent of £40 per annum for the first year rising to £70 per annum by the fourth year of operation. The depot was opened in October 1905 and received milk from the six Wensleydale stations and the small station of Sessay (not on the Wensleydale line). In its first year of operation milk was supplied to West Hartlepool and Newcastle but in 1906 milk was sent also to Sheffield and London.

There were, however, teething troubles and by 1908 the W.P.M.S. was in financial difficulties, possibly due to over expansion, a butter works and cheese room having been added to the depot in 1907. Farmers agreed to help the depot by receiving a drop in payment from 7½d to 7d per gallon which would save the Society £750 per annum. But the Society needed further help and asked the N.E.R. to reduce its freight charges on "gallons in cases" from 1½d to

1d to produce a further saving of £350 per annum. The N.E.R. agreed to lower the rates to keep the depot solvent. This was undoubtedly partly due to the fact that the receipts from the W.P.M.S. of over £1,800 per annum provided an appreciable proportion of the £15,000 total N.E.R. milk freight receipts in 1907.

The financial difficulties were resolved, therefore, and the W.P.M.S. flourished to the extent that in 1908 the N.E.R. provided a purpose built milk van for the Society. By 1911 the N.E.R. was able to report a substantial increase in receipts from milk co-operatives:

The most notable evidence is in the growth of forwardings of milk from Wensleydale since the establishment of the Wensleydale Pure Milk Society at Northallerton.

The W.P.M.S. enabled farmers to increase their milk output and by 1911 759,763 gallons were being forwarded annually from Wensleydale to the W.P.M.S. in Northallerton.

The N.E.R. report also noted that a co-operative had been formed at Redmire where the Wensleydale Farmers' Association Limited was establishing a dairy for cheese making and a facility for the transportation of whole milk in agreement with the N.E.R. from whom it leased land adjacent to the line at Redmire station. The lease stated that the premises to be built on the land should be used:

as a dairy or creamery preparing, manufacturing, selling and storing milk, butter, cream, eggs and cheese and such other farm products as may be previously approved in writing by the Company, as well as for receiving, storing and selling cake, manure, seed, flour, implements and other farm requisites approved by the Company.

The Redmire co-operative which had 50 members in 1911 was run in conjunction with the W.P.M.S. until it ceased trading in 1931. The following year the W.P.M.S. and the Redmire and West Burton Dairies were sold to the

Cow and Gate Company. The Northallerton depot continued to be worked and milk was forwarded by rail daily to the North East, Hull and two London depots, Queen's Park and Finsbury Park. In the 12 months from November 1936 approximately 654,000 gallons passed through the Northallerton depot to a total of 49 stations, though by this date only about 44,000 gallons were being despatched to the depot from Wensleydale. At no time did the depot receive all the Wensleydale milk.

Although liquid milk was produced in ever increasing quantities in the twentieth century, other dairy produce was not totally eclipsed and the railway greatly facilitated the movement of cheese, butter, cream and eggs from Wensleydale to Tyneside, Teesside, Hull, the West Riding and London. Empty butter boxes and cheese packing cases were returned from these places for re-use. The traffic was so important that in the early twentieth century the 3.25 p.m. Midland goods train from Hawes to Hawes Junction and Garsdale was instructed to wait on Tuesdays (market day) till 4 p.m. until the butter was ready for transportation. Dairy goods were not always transported without mishap and complaints were frequently received concerning damaged or wrongly invoiced goods. In 1881 out of a consignment of 65 cheeses sent from Askrigg to Bishop Auckland two were cracked. In the same year 31 cheeses were invoiced to Northallerton station but only 30 were received and, conversely, 199 cheeses were entered from Jaques and Knowles at Askrigg station but 214 were received at Stockton.

The 1920s and early 1930s saw the hey-day of rail milk traffic in Wensleydale. The roads became alive with activity each day when the milk carts rushed from farm to station to catch the milk trains. It was also a social occasion as people requested lifts from friends' milk carts to travel to different places in the dale. The farmers worked a rota system for loading all the deposited churns on to the waiting train. During harvest time, the farmers' wives delivered the milk and took great care to ensure that their ponies and carts were smartly "turned out" to impress the other women. Many minor mishaps occurred in the headlong dash to catch the train - one farmer's pony was so used to the journey that on one occasion it started off to the station without its master, delivering the milk on time and intact.

An analysis of accounts at Askrigg demonstrates the importance of the railway for dairy farmers. In 1925 Askrigg station held accounts for handling milk from 12 local farmers, from Mason's Dairy, Askrigg, and from Harper's Dairy, Bainbridge. Four years later Harper's Dairy closed which resulted in four more farmers forwarding their milk direct from the station. Other farmers opened accounts and by 1931 22 farmers in the area and Mason's Dairy had agreements with the London and North Eastern

Railway (L.N.E.R.), which had superseded the N.E.R. in 1923, to transport their milk. In that year Askrigg station forwarded 15,600 gallons to Leeds, 240,038 gallons to Finsbury Park and over 18,000 gallons to the Express Dairy at Appleby.

Unfortunately, changes in handling milk traffic were afoot which contributed to the eventual death of the railway. During September 1932, the last consignments of milk (amounting to 15,227 gallons for the month at Askrigg) passed through the upper dale stations. Most of this milk was forwarded to Appleby dairy. On 1 October, the milk lorries arrived in the dale and, with the exception of the Hawes area, took the milk direct from the farm to the dairy at Appleby. This traffic continued until January 1937 when an Express Dairy was opened at Leyburn and the upper dale's milk was transported there by motor lorry.

Milk churns being loaded at Redmire, circa 1920 or earlier. The engine lost its paint in the Hawes Junction fire in 1917. It was withdrawn in 1922. (K.A. Bell collection)

Milk train leaving Leyburn circa 1950. (J.W. Armstrong collection)

Initially, the milk cooling dairy at Leyburn employed eight people and handled 4,000 gallons of milk daily which was sent forward by rail to the Express Dairy's London bottling plant at Cricklewood. By the early 1950s 30 people were employed to handle the milk and some 33,000 gallons per day was being forwarded.

September 1932 was not quite the last time that milk was handled at the upper dale stations. In adverse weather conditions, such as the snowstorms which raged in February and March 1933, milk was again despatched by rail. During the five days when the lorries were snowbound, Askrigg Station forwarded 868 gallons to Cricklewood Dairy, 137 gallons to St. Pancras, and 2,537 gallons to Hawes Dairy.

A consideration of milk freight at Leyburn station between 1909 and 1939 demonstrates the importance of liquid milk not only as part of the agricultural economy of the dale but also in terms of revenue for the Wensleydale line. Milk traffic at the station increased dramatically from an annual average of 14,000 gallons in the early twentieth century over 304,000 gallons of milk in cans in 1925, including some 90,000 gallons destined for the W.P.M.S. By the mid 1930s much of the milk was being forwarded in specially constructed rail milk tanks. A peak for Leyburn was reached in 1939 when 3,227,215 gallons were moved in 1,227 tanks and a further 139,936 gallons were transported in 11,761 cans producing a total milk revenue for the L.N.E.R. at Leyburn of over £23,000. This amazing increase was due partly to the transference of most upper dale milk by motor lorry to Leyburn after 1937. The milk was forwarded by rail from Leyburn to Cricklewood until the closure of the passenger service in 1954. It was then moved by road to destinations in the north east and was only occasionally sent to Cricklewood (by road). Milk from the upper dale continued to be taken to Leyburn by lorry until the closure of the dairy in July 1970 and thereafter it was transferred to Wensleydale Creameries at Hawes for cheese and butter making.

The number of milk trains and vans transporting the milk varied with the life of the line. Until 1932 there was at least one N.E.R. (L.N.E.R. after 1922) milk train per day and, in addition, milk vans were attached to passenger trains. The special W.P.M.S. van was attached to the early passenger train and travelled daily, from Hawes initially, and later from Hawes Junction and Garsdale. Two other milk vans were each attached to the mid morning and early evening passenger trains from Hawes Junction and Garsdale. A single milk train ran on Sundays. Also during this period a special milk train departed daily from Wensleydale leaving Hawes at 7 p.m. with two milk vans from Hawes, two from Askrigg and one from Leyburn. This train arrived at King's Cross at 2.22 a.m. and at Finsbury Park depot at 2.55 a.m. The milk was then bottled for fresh delivery to the people of London. This traffic ceased in 1932 when the milk was transferred by motor lorry to Appleby. After 1932 only one daily milk train ran forward from Leyburn; this train ceased in 1954 when the line was closed to passengers. A substantial quantity of milk was sent by rail westwards with two morning trains departing daily from Hawes in the 1930s.

By the 1970s the dairy industry of the dale had come full circle from the pre-rail days of farm cheese and butter through the hey-day of liquid milk traffic to the factory cheese produced within the dale.

Mineral and stone traffic

Swaledale, and, to a lesser extent, Wensleydale had been centres for lead mining during the nineteenth century and railway promoters as early as the 1840s had claimed that a railway in the area would lead to the expansion of the industry. However, by the 1870s lead mining had entered its final decline and even the arrival of rail transport could not reverse the fortunes of industry. In 1881 less than 400 tons of lead was produced in Wensleydale and by 1893 production in the dale had ceased altogether. The industry survived slightly longer in adjacent Swaledale but the new Wensleydale railway was not used to transport the lead ore, which continued to be sent in the traditional manner due east direct to Teesside.

Some speculators in the 1870s had hoped that ironstone would be discovered and that the railway would enable a new industry to flourish. In 1876 several trial bores were sunk in the hills of the upper dale and some evidence of ironstone deposits was reputedly found but no further explorations were made.

However, the new railway did directly influence the rapid development of stone quarrying within the dale. Demand for stone was high in the expanding towns and cities and the potential which the railway offered Wensleydale for exporting stone was quickly recognised. Initially, the greatest impact was in the upper dale in the neighbourhood of Hawes where large deposits of good quality building stone, flags and slates had been discovered. A local writer in 1884 commented:

Since the introduction of the railway in its quiet valley [Wensleydale] ... flags, stones and mines are becoming valuable.

This was particularly true of two quarries near Burtersett which flourished after 1878. The two owners, Richard Metcalfe and Thomas Metcalfe, worked their quarries in intense and often acrimonious competition. Production at the two quarries rose from 6,180 tons in 1882 to nearly 13,000 tons in 1886. Other quarries in the district produced a further 3,000 tons in that year. Most of

top: Wensley mineral ropeway top station, from the top of the new hopper.(M. Scarr)

above: Gantry and hopper. (M. Scarr)

left: Overhead cableway with limestone from quarry. Note the stone wagons waiting below in sidings just outside Wensley station. (P. Moore collection)

survive despite the fall in demand. However, in 1916 Richard Metcalfe, who had the larger quarry, suffered bankruptcy and a company was formed to run the quarry. During the same period Tom Metcalfe's quarry was managed first by his son and then by his son-in-law. The later years of the First World War brought further disruption and attendant financial problems, so that by the 1920s the industry was virtually dead and Tom Metcalfe's quarry closed. Richards Metcalfe's quarry was sold to a Durham mining engineer who struggled to survive but finally closed the quarry in the 1930s.

In enabling this industry to flourish, albeit for a short period, the railway directly influenced employment prospects for a number of local people who would probably otherwise have had to leave the area in search of work. In 1882 over 80 people worked in the quarries of the upper dale and the numbers employed rose rapidly to reach a peak of nearly 200 towards the end of the decade. Although the industry went into a sustained decline, it still employed in excess of 100 people at the turn of the century.

In periods of high demand Burtersett quarries alone were sending 80 tons of stone per day to Hawes in four large, two-horse, purpose built stone wagons each of which often made four trips a day down the steep hill from the village to the station. The wagons were constructed with special brakes called "slippers" to prevent the five-ton loads of stone from running out of control on the steep road.

Whereas the upper dale stone industry had flourished in the late nineteenth century and then quickly died, the quarry industry of the lower dale developed slowly in the nineteenth century, after the opening of Leyburn station but expanded rapidly in response to demand in the early twentieth century. The quarries of the lower dale were primarily limestone and so supplied a different market from that of the building trade which the sandstone

Mineral sidings on the western outskirts of Leyburn. (K.A. Bell)

the stone was forwarded westward on the Midland network, presumably to industrial Lancashire and probably the Burnley and Colne areas. Some of the stone was sent to London where, reputedly, one of its uses was as casings for manhole covers for the capital's sewerage system.

In 1879, the Midland Company forwarded 2,664 tons of stone from Hawes station and by 1889, when at least six quarries in the area were in operation, over 13,000 tons of stone freight was carried on the Midland line. The N.E.R. also forwarded an unspecified, but probably quite small tonnage, on its line. The peak of the upper dale stone industry occurred in the late 1880s and although quarrying continued to thrive during the 1890s, demand fell at the turn of the century. By 1903 both the Burtersett owners had experienced financial difficulties but managed to

quarries of the upper dale served. The carboniferous limestones of Wensleydale were quarried mainly for aggregate and for flux in the steel industry.

Initially, the limestone traffic from the lower dale was small. A siding to serve Harmby Quarry, immediately east of Leyburn, had been constructed when the railway was built in 1856 and limestone from that quarry was recorded in Leyburn traffic ledgers in the 1860s. Agreements between the quarry owners and the N.E.R. were modified periodically. In 1908 Siddall Bros., the quarry owners signed an agreement which was further extended in 1911. Also in 1911 Ord and Maddison Ltd. of Darlington drew up an agreement with the N.E.R. concerning sidings at West Quarry on the outskirts of Leyburn. This quarry had been in operation since the nineteenth century and by 1914 was producing 14,000 tons per annum. Two other quarries, at Redmire and Wensley, were also forwarding limestone by rail in the early twentieth century.

Demand for limestone fluctuated wildly and during some years output from the quarries was exceptionally high. As early as 1875 over 28,700 tons was forwarded from Leyburn, which handled the traffic from Harmby and West Quarry. In the immediate post-war period demand fell until in the 1920s a recovery in the industry led to a dramatic rise in output. Limestone freight forwarded from Leyburn leapt from 11,000 tons in 1920 to 44,000 in 1927. Surprisingly, during this period production declined at West Quarry. Further west, however, Redmire Limestone Quarry Ltd. expanded rapidly and in 1920 the Company signed an agreement with the N.E.R. concerning the installation of a siding at Redmire station for the stone traffic from the quarry. Production at the quarry rose rapidly from 11,000 tons in 1921 to over 33,000 tons in 1923. The South Durham Steel and Iron Company, which owned Wensley Limestone Quarry Ltd., signed an agreement with the N.E.R. in 1922 regarding sidings to service the quarry, and production here also increased.

Limestone output declined between 1928 and 1933. However, this was followed by another period of expansion and in 1934 over 47,000 tons was forwarded from Leyburn. Thereafter production continued to fluctuate but, gradually, continuous decline ensued. Between the Second World War and the 1990s all the quarries, with the exception of Redmire, had ceased production.

Gannister, a close grained stone used primarily to line steel furnaces, was produced intermittently in the dale and forwarded by rail in the late nineteenth and early twentieth centuries. In 1888 over 5,000 tons was exported from the upper dale but by 1893 output had ceased. In 1920 gannister was again in demand and in that year 500 tons were forwarded from Askrigg and nearly 4,000 tons from Wensley. Although there is no further indication of gannister quarrying it probably continued to be produced at intervals.

The number of trains carrying mineral freight varied according to demand. In the early part of the twentieth century one mineral train ran daily serving West Quarry and Harmby Quarry. From 1922 this train was scheduled to run daily from Tuesday to Saturday. In periods of high demand two mineral trains served the Redmire and Wensley quarries daily but when demand fell one mineral train per day carried this freight. In the late nineteenth and early twentieth century mineral trains ran from Hawes over the Midland system.

Coal traffic

Before the railway era local people used either peat from the moors or coal which was extracted locally or brought from further afield. Durham and other quality coal was transported into the dale first by packhorse and later by wagon. This imported coal was expensive but was of much better quality than the local dales' coal. For example, in 1846 the price of coal per ton in Wensleydale was 27s but at London Dock Side it was only 16s 10d per ton. The people of Wensleydale hoped that, with the arrival of the railway, the better quality coal would be more easily obtainable and also that it would be more reasonably priced. Immediately the line opened to Hawes, increased competition led to a fall in prices. Prior to 1 August 1878 good quality coal sold at 9d per hundredweight but within days of the rail service commencing one dealer reduced his coal to 8½d, another lowered his Newland, Wallsend's best, to 8d and a third dealer, a newcomer to the trade, offered his coal at 7d. A week later, one of the dealers was advertising his St. John's, Normanton, coal at 6½d per hundredweight including delivery within Hawes town.

Other dales people were not so fortunate. A heated argument developed in the early 1860s about the price of South Durham coal at Leyburn. Rather than decreasing since the opening of the station it appears that the price of coal actually increased. However, eventually prices settled down in the dale and in 1880 when the price of a ton of coal in Wensley was 10s, the best coal at London Dock Side was 14s 11d per ton.

Coal traffic on the railway was substantial. Between 1856 and 1877 Leyburn station received all the coal for delivery to upper Wensleydale, amounting to about 11,000 tons per annum. After 1877, when Leyburn station served only its immediate hinterland an average of 5,000 tons per annum were received. Most of the coal was sold through the station depot and became known as "station coal". Some, however, was forwarded to special consignees. Harmby Quarry, for example, received an average of 200 tons per annum in the early twentieth century. Small quantities of coke were also sold through the depot and some was specially consigned to the local gas works at Leyburn which had been established when the railway opened in 1856. By the 1930s coal traffic at the station had decreased to 3,087 tons per annum of which 2,819 tons were for domestic use and 268 tons for industrial purposes.

The six N.E.R. stations in the early twentieth century received a total of between 11,000 and 13,000 tons of coal per annum and, approximately, a further 1,700 tons were received annually over the Midland branch line.

Miscellaneous goods traffic

Wensleydale had largely been denuded of its timber long before the arrival of the railway so it is somewhat surprising that timber freight was forwarded by rail in the twentieth century. The timber was carried by purpose-built wagons from the felling area to the local stations where it was lifted on to rail timber trucks by crane. The heavy logs were not easy to transport along the narrow country lanes and at least one bad accident occurred. In about 1910 timber was being carried to Aysgarth station via Aysgarth Falls. The driver lost control of the horses and wagon on the steep hill down to the river and the load careered down the hill and crashed through the wall into the falls. In 1906, 700 tons of timber were forwarded from the N.E.R. stations. This traffic increased to 1,959 tons in 1920 and continued to rise until towards the end of the decade. Thereafter, little timber was felled and the railway was only very occasionally used for transporting wood.

Another surprising commodity exported from the dale was flour. Apart from during the war years no corn had been grown in the upper dales since the early nineteenth century. Several corn mills were still operating in the early twentieth century but all the corn was imported and was usually ground solely for local consumption. However, Aysgarth and, to a lesser extent, Askrigg sent flour and meal forward from the dale.

Originally built as a cotton mill, Yore Mills at Aysgarth Falls ground corn from the late nineteenth century. No corn was ground for a decade from 1927 but in the late 1930s Yorkshire Farmers Ltd. restarted milling and continued grinding corn until 1959. Thereafter it was used as a provender mill. In 1964 Yorkshire Farmers Ltd. was taken

No 62044 on Goods train passing Redmire. (N.E. Stead)

over by West Cumberland Farmers Trading Society and Yore Mills continued in production until its final closure in the 1970s. As early as April 1877 large quantities of corn were being delivered by rail to Aysgarth station. In that month over 44 tons of maize were sent from Teesside, Tyneside and Liverpool, of which 24 tons were destined for Yore Mills and 20 tons for local farmers. Yore Mills also received 27 tons of wheat that month. In the early years of the twentieth century an average of 300 tons of flour was being forwarded annually from Aysgarth station by Yore Mills.

During the early twentieth century Askrigg station was forwarding an average of 100 tons of flour annually in addition to animal cake and meal. In the early 1920s Askrigg station regularly received five-ton consignments of grain via the Hull and Barnsley Railway from Alexandra Dock, Hull, and from Spillers and Bakers via Newcastle Forth Station.

Goods received into the dale were almost as vital to the economy of the area as goods forwarded. Invoices available for Aysgarth station for April 1877 present a graphic picture of the amount and variety of goods received at the new station in one month. Apart from the corn noted above, farmers received over four tons of oats, two tons of potatoes, twelve tons of hay, three tons of straw and seven and a half tons of manure which were sent from the Alum Company at Middlesborough. Other items received included a drill, a cheese press and two harrows. During April, 219 empty butter boxes, mainly from the Midland Station at Bradford, were returned to Aysgarth dairy farmers for re-use.

Building activity in the Aysgarth area in April 1877 was quite intense and substantial quantities of building materials arrived at the station during the month. Mr Yeo, a Redmire builder, received over eight tons of deals via Stockton Station, six tons of slates via Middlesbrough Station, 30,000 bricks from Thirsk, and 42-hundredweight

bags of plaster from Cumwhinton near Carlisle. Local joiners, J. Chandler and Son, were employed at Aysgarth Vicarage and, in addition to miscellaneous building materials, received over two tons of wood. Several individuals received door and window frames and large quantities of laths. Nine hundredweight of glass was received by two customers and Thomas Shield, tinner of Castle Bolton, received three sheets of zinc iron weighing a hundredweight.

Provisions arriving at Aysgarth in April 1877 included boxes of soap, chests of sugar and tea, and casks of syrup for shopkeepers. A three-hundredweight crate of whiting from Stockton was invoiced via Aysgarth station to a Burtersett shopkeeper. Fresh sea fish for the first time could be brought easily into the dale and local people quickly welcomed this addition to their diet. (In 1881, Askrigg received barrels of herrings from Tynemouth and several consignments of fish from Grimsby, Lowestoft and Morecambe).

During April 1877 wines and spirits arrived at Aysgarth in substantial quantities and 207 gallons of ale were received, of which 107 gallons had been forwarded from Bass & Co. of Burton via the Midland railway. The wealthier residents of the dale received luxury items. Two three-hundredweight casks of "petro oil", one from Newcastle, the other from Birkenhead, arrived at the station. The vicar of Aysgarth was the recipient of one of these casks. A box of china was sent "with care" from Doncaster to Mr Sadler of Thoralby and Robert Lodge, a substantial Bishopdale landowner, received a large picture.

Commodities were received in Wensleydale not only from all parts of this country but also from abroad via the ports of the North. Cider was sent from Leominster, salt from Norwich, Welsh slates from Bangor, Llangollen and Dolgellau, common slates from Windermere, concrete blocks from Lancashire, cement from the Midlands, sanitary pipes from Castleton, soot (for lightening the soil)

Wensleydale line freight traffic, weekdays circa 1904

		Mail	Coal	Goods	Midland Goods	(3) Goods	(4) Goods
		a.m.	a.m.	a.m.	p.m.	p.m.	p.m.
Northallerton	dep.	4.40	7.05	7.50	-	1.45	3.40
Leyburn	arr.	5.15	10.00	11.00	-	3.30	6.35
Leyburn	dep.	-	-	11.00	-	-	-
Wensley		-	-	A	-	-	-
Redmire		-	-	A	-	-	-
Aysgarth		5.29	-	1.40	-	-	-
Askrigg		5.38	-	A	-	-	-
Hawes	arr.	5.47	-	2.15	-	-	-
Hawes	dep.	-	-	-	3.25	-	-
Hawes Junction	arr.	-	-	-	3.45	-	-

		(1) Empty B	(2) Cattle BC	Mineral	Midland Goods	Goods	(3) Goods	(4) Goods
		a.m.	a.m.	a.m.	p.m.	p.m.	p.m.	p.m.
Hawes Junction	dep.	-	-	-	1.55	-	-	-
Hawes		6.00	6.20	-	2.15	3.15	-	-
Askrigg		6.08	6.32	-	-	3.35	-	-
Aysgarth		6.16	6.46	-	-	4.10	-	-
Redmire		-	7.00	-	-	A	-	-
Wensley		-	-	-	-	A	-	-
Leyburn	arr.	6.30	7.10	-	-	4.40	-	-
Leyburn	dep.	6.32	7.20	11.50	-	5.15	5.25	7.45
Northallerton	arr.	7.04	9.30	2.35	-	6.20	7.20	9.11

A - stops if required. B – horse boxes and carriage trucks to be sent by this train. C – a third class carriage is attached to this train for the accommodation of men in charge of stock
(1) - except Tuesday
(2) - Tuesdays only
(3) - does not run Mondays, Tuesdays and alternate Thursdays
(4) – runs every Monday, Tuesday and alternate Thursdays

from Glasgow and Edinburgh, basic slag (for spreading on the pastures) from Middlesbrough, iron and steel from Teesside, and deals, battens and boards from Hartlepool.

During the early twentieth century extensive road improvements were undertaken and the required materials were received in large quantities. In 1923 2,000 tons of tarred slag and chippings arrived in eight-ton truck loads at Askrigg station from Stockton. The consignment was to be divided between Askrigg and Hawes. And in 1927 4,000 tons of untarred roadstone were forwarded from Leyburn to Askrigg.

After the opening of the railway, dales people enjoyed an improvement in their mail service. In 1878 Hawes Post Office announced that a second daily delivery and despatch of mail was to be introduced. Mail was to be forwarded on the 7.50 a.m. and 4.50 p.m. passenger trains and incoming mail would arrive on the 9.25 a.m. and 6.35 p.m. trains. By the early twentieth century a special daily mail train was run into the dale arriving at Hawes at 5.47 a.m. Apart from carrying outgoing mail the train was to run back empty unless there were any horse boxes or cattle trucks to be attached.

Goods traffic on the Wensleydale line increased dramatically in the years following the opening and rose to a peak of over 25,000 tons in 1898. The traffic then settled to an annual average of 20,000 tons prior to the First World War but fell during the hostilities when non-essential goods movement was kept to a minimum. There was a slight recovery in the 1920s but thereafter the rail service was gradually superseded by motor transport and goods traffic declined steadily until the line closed.

The number of freight trains working the line varied according to demand. During the life of the line at least one regular return goods train ran daily from Northallerton to Hawes. In the early twentieth century a second return goods train ran as far as Leyburn. Coal usually arrived on the goods train but occasionally special coal trains were provided. In addition, the daily mineral train from Leyburn was instructed to carry forward important perishable traffic and cattle when required. For a period in the late 1920s six freight trains, including return movements were stopping daily at Leyburn. This volume of traffic was not maintained and by the 1950s apart from the mineral trains, only the one daily return goods train served Leyburn and the upper dale. The Midland Company also ran at least one daily goods train on its branch.

The N.E.R. employed carriers in the locality of its stations to collect and deliver small goods and parcels. These carriers worked under strict agreements with the N.E.R. In 1898, Henry Kilding of Leyburn was hired to carry parcels, goods and other articles, including passengers' luggage, within one mile of the station. Under the terms of the agreement he was to be paid 1s 8d per ton.

Occasionally, parcels and goods were lost in transit. In 1875 an Aysgarth draper despatched a woollen suit, 14 yards of silk and other articles valued at £9 12s 8d from Leyburn station to a gentleman in Newcastle. The parcel failed to arrive. Police later discovered the articles in a pawnshop and traced the culprit, a porter at Newcastle Central Station. In 1881 Pickfords and Company of Leeds complained that two bottles of wine had been pilfered between Askrigg and Leeds and claimed four shillings compensation from the N.E.R.

Station receipts

Total station receipts on the Wensleydale line were not high and it is doubtful if the line ever made a substantial profit. Receipts at the N.E.R. stations rose from about £13,000 in the 1890s to an early twentieth century peak of over £17,000 per annum. After the First World War the increase in milk traffic boosted revenue at the six stations until 1932 when, with the exception of Leyburn, the milk traffic ceased. Thereafter total receipts fell annually until the closure of the line.

The table below page of Leyburn traffic receipts between 1868 and 1939 demonstrates the shifting emphasis of sources of revenue.

Although Leyburn station appears to have been in a financially healthy position in the inter-war period, the bulk of its revenue was from two sources, minerals and milk. By the 1930s its mineral traffic, which was not recorded in 1939, was in decline and its increase in milk traffic was at the expense of the other Wensleydale stations. On the eve of the Second World War, Leyburn, in common with other stations, was rapidly losing both its passengers and parcels to motor transport.

The impact of the railway

It is not possible to identify precisely the impact that the railway had on the economy and society of Wensleydale and upper Swaledale. In general terms, the railway opened up the dale to the mainstream influences of Victorian England and enabled dales people easily to export their produce to the rest of the country. Specifically, the railway helped the growth of tourism and enabled farmers to adapt their farming and find new markets. The railway did not achieve its peak impact on all sectors of the economy at the same time. For example, freight traffic such as cattle, sandstone, coal and goods reached their peak level in the late nineteenth century, while for sheep and passengers the peak was between 1901 and 1925, and for milk, limestone and race horses the peak was reached between 1926 and 1954.

The Wensleydale railway arrived, in one sense, in the 'nick of time'. The 1870s marked the beginning of a period when the dales, along with other areas in the country, were suffering from falling prices and an increasingly depressed economy. In order to survive, the dales needed an improved form of transport that would enable local industries to compete in the national market place.

Unfortunately, the railway itself, despite the boost it gave to the local economy, was not enough to stop the decline in population. In fact, although it brought

Leyburn traffic receipts

	Passengers	Parcels	Horses Carriages Dogs	Livestock	Goods	Total Receipts
	£	£	£	£	£	£
1868	2762	1260		386	2480	6888
1888	2863	362	1066	864	1844	6999
1908	2826	2431[1]		524	2242	8023
1928	4416	748	6366[2]	287	9457[3]	21,274
1939	1898	325	25,800[2]	Not recorded		28,023[4]

[1] probably includes milk revenue
[2] includes milk traffic revenue
[3] includes mineral traffic revenue
[4] when miscellaneous coaching traffic is included the total is £32,905

advantages, paradoxically the railway helped the decline both by increasing mobility and awareness of the outside world and by aiding mass-produced articles to enter the dale and thereby adversely affect the local craft industries.

The railway was also unlikely to have been very profitable for the N.E.R. and Midland companies though at times certain classes of traffic such as passengers, stone and milk probably far exceeded expectations. It is most likely that the main reason for building the line was to protect what the N.E.R. and Midland Companies saw as their territory from rival claims and that high profitability was not the major issue. As a branch line in a relatively remote rural area, it was probably only occasionally profitable and overall cannot have provided reasonable return on the capital invested - although the line did contribute "onward" traffic to the main lines of both companies.

Horsebox at Leyburn Station circa 1950.
(WRA collection)

8 The end of an era

By the early 1950s the Wensleydale line was reputedly losing over £14,000 per annum. Proposals to close the line to passenger traffic were announced by the British Transport Commission (B.T.C.) in 1954 and were met by a storm of protest from local people and railway enthusiasts. The protest had little chance of being effective as it was estimated that only 2½ per cent of dales residents used the line. Local people acknowledged that often, particularly in the post-war period, the passenger trains had carried only a handful of people. Nevertheless strong representations were made to retain the service with claims that the closure would be damaging to the economy of the dale and that the B.T.C. had made no serious attempt to attract passengers. In the 1950s, apart from the few months immediately prior to the announcement of the closure proposals, no cheap tickets had been issued and as the

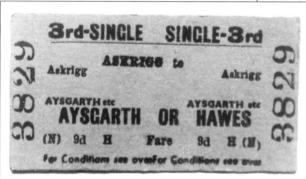

above: Ticket for last passenger train 24 April 1954. (M. Hartley)

right: Last passenger train arriving at Askrigg, 1954. (M. Hartley)

No 62347 at Hawes on the final day of the full passenger service, 24 April 1954. (N.E. Stead collection)

train's fare from Northallerton to Wensleydale was double the bus fare there was little incentive to travel by rail. The battle to save the service was eventually lost and the North Eastern Area Transport Users' Consultative Committee approved the closure plans. Apart from the impact on passengers, the closure of the line affected the jobs of some 50 railway personnel.

The final day of the full passenger service was Saturday, 24 April 1954 and the last return train to Garsdale departed from Northallerton at 4.10 p.m. There was a carnival atmosphere among the young people but the elderly felt a sense of loss at the passing of an old friend. Although "Old Faithful", the 53-year old Darlington built

tank engine, was not pulling the train, the local people turned out in force to pay their last respects. Over 200 people travelled the complete four-hour journey. A party of 40 dales people booked a special coach from Leyburn and took a "funeral feast" of beer and food to keep up their spirits during the journey! The vicar of Redmire, the Rev D. T. Reynolds Carlin, completed the funereal atmosphere by placing a wreath inscribed "Goodbye Old Faithful" on the funnel of the J21 engine no. 65038. As a further mark of respect black crepe bands were attached to the rear carriages.

The train rested for 45 minutes at Garsdale before making the final journey to Northallerton. During the

Last passenger train at Garsdale. (J.W. Armstrong)

return trip crowds lined the route and Union Jacks and black flags were flown at half mast in the villages of the dale. At Hawes 80 people in hopeful optimism bought return tickets to Northallerton. Between Bainbridge and Askrigg a large notice was displayed which read: "Death of a veteran Old Faithful R.I.P."

The following day the last passenger train to Leyburn made the round trip from Northallerton in two hours, this time linked up with the genuine "Old Faithful" engine which had "Your Last Run" chalked on its side. The engine pulled a milk tanker and one coach with only 16 passengers - mainly rail enthusiasts who had missed the previous day's excitement.

So ended the era of passenger trains in Wensleydale. Sadly it was a very brief span of only 76 years, so short in fact that one of the final passengers, 84 year old Mrs Margaret Horner from Askrigg, remembered seeing the first passenger train arrive in the dale in 1877. The passenger service between Garsdale and Hawes survived for another six years until 16 March 1959, when the old Midland (later London, Midland and Scottish - after 1923) branch line was also closed.

Although the full passenger service had ceased, occasional passenger trains travelled the dale for a few more years. On 4 May 1955 a Rail Tour excursion was run over the line and during the bad weather of 1962/3, in response to an earlier promise, the passenger service was resumed in January for a few days. Ten years after the passenger closure the Railway Correspondence and Travel Society organised a commemorative excursion on 25 April 1964. As the line west of Redmire was completely closed immediately after that date this excursion was the last passenger train to travel the full length of the line. A further excursion as far as Redmire took place when a steam-hauled train travelled from Stockton on 20 May 1967.

Workers lift the track near Askrigg, 1965. (K.A. Bell)

The goods service was closed at Aysgarth, Askrigg and Hawes on 27 April 1964; at Wensley on 3 July 1967; and at Leyburn in 1969. Leyburn and Redmire stations remained open as unmanned public delivery sidings. This facility was closed at Leyburn in 1982. With the termination of the goods service Wensleydale lost the facility of convenience and speed that the railway had afforded the movement of freight to and from the dale.

The line after closure

In 1965 the track west of Redmire was removed and many of the bridges demolished. In 1964 the National Trust considered acquiring the whole length of the disused Wensleydale line, from Redmire to Garsdale for use as a recreational footpath. The Trust decided against acquisition, however, being deterred by British Railways' stipulation "that any purchaser would have to take over all responsibility for the future maintenance of fences, walls, ditches, culverts, bridges, level crossings etc ...". The idea of acquiring the line for use as a public footpath was resurrected in 1966, this time by the former North Riding County Council. By then the Hawes to Garsdale branch line

Dismantling the one railway bridge which spanned the River Ure between Hawes and Bainbridge, 1965. (K.A. Bell)

had been sold off to the adjoining landowners. The North Riding County Council decided to take no action concerning the purchase of the line, influenced primarily by the extensive liabilities for which it would have been obliged to assume responsibility. A final attempt to acquire the line for use as a recreational footpath was made in 1970-71, when the North Riding County Council considered the acquisition of the line between Redmire and Aysgarth. The majority of this stretch had either been sold off or contracted for sale already and the Council again decided not to proceed with the proposal. Almost all of the line west of Redmire has now reverted to agricultural use and is in private ownership. At certain points, however, public footpaths cross over the line or travel adjacent to it, so it is possible for today's visitor to sample the views experienced in former times by the rail travellers.

Until recently the railway remained open for mineral traffic from Redmire Quarry that provided flux for the Teesside steel industry. The daily train carried 800 tons of ground limestone in 23 wagons. When demand was high, two trains were run daily.

An excursion train stands ready to return to Northallerton, April 1964. (K.A. Bell)

The line as far as Redmire was used occasionally for passengers. The Yorkshire Dales National Park Committee ran its first experimental "Dales Rail" train between Newcastle and Redmire on Saturday, 17 September 1977. The train stopped at Durham, Darlington, Bedale and Leyburn and was hired at a cost of £900. The diesel engine pulled six carriages, which had a total capacity of 345 seats, and made two double journeys that both brought visitors to the area and took dales people to Newcastle. On that day 138 visitors travelled by rail into the dale and 319 local people visited Newcastle. Buses were provided to link the service with upper Wensleydale and Swaledale. Following this successful venture, the experiment was continued in 1978 with service on two days. In June a seven-car diesel operated from Leeds and York and in September a six car diesel ran from Newcastle. The service was run twice yearly in 1979 and 1980 but the last such

excursion took place on Saturday, 20th April 1981. An eight-car diesel with a capacity of 400 seats travelled a double return journey from York to Redmire. Demand from York was not great but a total of 342 people (170 adults, 75 O.A.Ps, and 97 children) travelled from Redmire. The return tickets for adults cost £2.90. Because of lack of demand at York British Rail declined to run any further trains. Since autumn 1981 occasional trains have been run, both by British Rail, to destinations including Saltburn, and by private charter companies.

Although the Wensleydale railway is closed to regular passenger trains and the track west of Redmire removed, the stations from Leyburn westwards still remain and serve a variety of purposes. The station house at Leyburn and the nearby station buildings are used for a variety of industrial and domestic purposes.

Limestone train at Redmire. (N.E. Stead)

Train No 46475 arrives at Askrigg from Aysgarth in the bad winter of 1963 when snow-blocked roads briefly forced the re-opening of the passenger service – a salutary reminder of the invaluable lifeline which the railway offered to people living in the dale. (K.A. Bell)

Wensley station buildings were transferred to Lord Bolton's ownership after the closure. Initially the station was let as a private house, but after a number of years the property was sold. Redmire station office has, unfortunately, been demolished but the station master's house has been extended and is used as a scout centre. The small dairy nearby is used for storage and a workshop. The two railway workers' cottages have been converted to a house and is privately owned, as are most of the cottages along the line.

The station building at Aysgarth was converted and modernised to form two private houses. The area to the west of the station was developed by the Yorkshire Dales National Park Committee (now Authority) to create a large car park and the nearby railway workers' cottages have been converted and extended to accommodate a National Park Centre and café.

Askrigg station was internally gutted and rebuilt and was the office of T.W.Weatherald Ltd., a local building firm.

No 62347 on the Garsdale turntable which fell into disuse after the final closure of the line. In 1989 it was removed to Keighley where it is now working on the Keighley and Worth Valley Railway. (J.W. Armstrong collection)

This firm also owned the goods warehouse and other buildings at the station. In 2000 Weatherald Wood Components Ltd took over the firm and the station site.

The station yard at Hawes was acquired by the Yorkshire Dales National Park Authority and laid out as a car park, providing much needed parking space for visitors during the summer months. The Derby Gothic station building was altered internally to form a National Park Centre. The large goods warehouse was renovated and leased to the County's Libraries and Museums Committee to accommodate the excellent Upper Dales Folk Museum. In order to house the increasing number of museum exhibits, a covered extension has been built which joins the goods warehouse to the station building, thereby creating the new Dales Countryside Museum which combines the National Park Centre and tourist information with the museum. The up-platform shelter is a National Park Wardens' workshop and store. The nearby station master's house is privately owned. The platform shelters at Garsdale are still in use as waiting rooms for passengers on the Settle-Carlisle line and as storage depots for Network Rail. In order to deal with the recent increase in freight traffic as well as passenger trains on the Settle-Carlisle line, the Garsdale signal box has now been fully reopened.

Apart from the demolished Redmire station offices, all the buildings on the Wensleydale line retain much of their original appearance and provide a timely reminder of a bygone period when the railway was a vital part of the dale's life.

9 Developments since the 1980s

During the 1980s a few excursion trains were run into Wensleydale and the daily freight trains continued to take limestone from Redmire to Teesside. Interest nationally in old railways was growing and within Wensleydale a small group of people began to consider the implications of reinstating the full Wensleydale railway line. An impetus to these discussions was the increasing pressure on local roads from tourist traffic. By the early 1990s, for example, the main Wensleydale road (A684) was carrying over two million tourist journeys per annum. Further, the reprieve of the Settle-Carlisle line in 1989 meant that there still remained links to connect the Wensleydale line to both the west and the east rail networks.

Discussions about the Wensleydale line remained informal until Ruth Annison, a Hawes businesswoman, organised an exploratory meeting of interested people. At their meeting on 26 March 1990, the small group decided to take matters forward in a more active and concerted manner. On 23 May 1990, at a public meeting in Redmire, the Wensleydale Railway Association (WRA) was formed with a view to exploring the possibility of reopening the 40-mile railway line throughout Wensleydale to once again link the main East Coast line with the Settle-Carlisle line. The realisation of this aim to restore the line to its former status would require reinstating the 18 miles (Redmire to Garsdale) that had been finally closed and track lifted in 1964. It was felt that the line would improve communication within and beyond Wensleydale for local people and tourists alike and thus, as in its former heyday, enable an injection of resources into the dales area. The first WRA officers were County Councillor John Piper (Chairman), Alan Barrett (Treasurer), Ruth Annison (Secretary), Irene Bergerud (Membership), and Stan Abbott (Press Officer). There were also seven other committee members (including Scott Handley).

The project was, and is, a mammoth one. Even in 1990 a survey undertaken by British Rail estimated that, despite the generally good condition of the infrastructure, the cost of reinstating the 18 mile missing link would be as much as £1 million per mile. The replacement of the bridge over the Ure near Hawes, for example, was estimated to cost about £2 million. However, the vision and dedication of those early members of the WRA[1] has meant that the Association expanded rapidly in membership and resources. In order to identify and prioritise the work that was needed to achieve their aim, the WRA raised funds to undertake a feasibility study of the line. On the basis of that study the WRA, fully aware of the scale of the project, decided to go ahead. Over the next couple of years, as the WRA was expanding rapidly in several directions, there was a need to create separate 'arms' for the different operations. In 1992 'The Wensleydale Railway Company Ltd.' (now TWRC Ltd) was formed and related Company activities included trading, property and rolling stock. Subsequently, provision was made for charitable donations and Gift Aid via the Wensleydale Railway

Ruth Annison, Founder Member of the WRA. (Nigel Whitfield, Darlington & StocktonTimes 4.7.03)

[1] Note: there are a number of companies that have been established in order to deal with specific aspects of the WRA's original aims and objectives. In this chapter the use of 'WRA' or 'WR' also covers the activities of the separate companies.

Leeming Bar circa 1960. (N.E. Stead)

Trust. During the last decade the Association has faced many challenges but, against all the odds, has also enjoyed some remarkable successes.

An early problem with which the WRA had to deal was Yorkshire Water's proposal to lay, where feasible, its new Wensleydale water main along the old trackbed route. After lengthy negotiations with Yorkshire Water the WRA received assurances that when the line was reopened the route of the pipeline would be moved away from the trackbed. Having successfully overcome that problem a further blow came in September 1992. British Steel announced that it was transferring transport of its Redmire limestone from rail to road. After a protracted campaign by local people and others, including a parliamentary petition led by William Hague MP, to keep limestone transport on the railway, British Steel decided to close the Redmire quarry and use Cumbrian quarried limestone instead. The future looked very grim for the WRA as, inevitably, the 22-mile line from Northallerton to Redmire would be closed and the track dismantled. This would mean that the whole of the Wensleydale line from Northallerton to Garsdale

would be totally disused. The final limestone freight train from Redmire to Teesside ran on 18 December 1992. Such was the dismay at the decision to close the existing railway that no fewer than three special passenger trains were run over the line during its final days. The last train, which was full to capacity with over 720 people, was the 13-coach diesel chartered by Hertfordshire Rail Tours. The train, which, with echoes of the 1954 closure, was dubbed the 'Wensleydale Lament', left Kings Cross on January 2 1993 at 7.40 a.m. and arrived at Redmire at 1.30 p.m.

British Rail decided to sell the Northallerton to Redmire line which it valued at £1.1 million pounds and bids were invited. The WRA saw no alternative but to attempt to buy the line which had been independently valued at about half the British Rail valuation. A campaign to raise funds by issuing 'track units' was launched on 15 March 1993. The situation was made more fraught both by a Pickering businessman who stated that he was putting in a bid and then, just before bidding closed, by a third, anonymous bidder who entered the fray. By September 1993 when the bids had to be submitted to British Rail, the WRA had raised over £75,000. As members of the WRA anxiously awaited

MoD moving tanks by rail on the Wensleydale line, late 1990s. (Michael Bentley)

the outcome, the story took another twist. British Rail announced that, in the light of other potential developments, it was withdrawing the line from offer of sale.

The reprieve for the existing line had come from an unexpected source. The Ministry of Defence (MoD) expressed an interest in using the railway in order to avoid the busy A1 road when moving tanks between Salisbury Plain and the large army base at Catterick Garrison a few miles from Redmire. Throughout the negotiations the WRA worked in close co-operation with the MoD and other involved parties. The MoD ran a trial train in November 1993 and the decision to go ahead with the project was eventually taken in 1995. The MoD invested £750,000 in upgrading the Northallerton to Redmire section in preparation for what was hoped to be a regular usage by the army. A test train ran on the line in April 1996, with full MoD operations commencing in July. The reprieve came just in time as the track was beginning to get seriously overgrown and was in urgent need of maintenance. In an important subsidiary development the WRA gained the support of the MoD for its plans to reinstate passenger services.

The initiatives undertaken by the WRA and the fortuitous involvement of the MoD meant that there was increased interest in the Wensleydale line nationally and this helped the rapid expansion of the WRA. Several WRA branches were established in different parts of the country, including a London Branch. The fund-raising initiative of issuing 'track units' proved to be very successful and 1,659 units had been issued by June 1997 when the track unit fund stood at £107,255. With this consolidation of membership and increasing financial resources, the WRA was able to push forward its aim of reinstating the whole of the Wensleydale line.

The WRA decided that the first phase of achieving its objectives would be the purchase and re-laying of track between Redmire and Castle Bolton. In 1997 the WRA was

successful in purchasing both 650 metres of usable trackbed between the MoD Redmire railhead and 600 metres of trackbed that it had earlier leased from the Bolton estate. Before this section of the line can be fully reconstructed a new bridge has to be built over Apedale beck between Redmire and Castle Bolton. By summer 1999 the Association was involved in further negotiation with the Bolton Estate to lease another substantial section of trackbed between Bolton Castle and Aysgarth. In order to complete its control of the track between Redmire and Aysgarth Falls, the WRA also purchased the remainder of Railtrack's holding on this section of the line. This means the WRA controls the majority of the former trackbed between Redmire and Aysgarth Falls. All these initiatives came at a cost. By May 1999 c.£750,000 had been invested by the WRA in Leyburn, Castle Bolton and Aysgarth and since that date investment has continued as more resources have become available.

Although the WRA works to a carefully constructed list of priorities, these can be subject to change when other opportunities arise. For example, during 1997 about three acres at Aysgarth station including the goods shed, signalling cabin and other buildings, became available. Finance to assist in purchasing this came from the next WRA fund-raising scheme, the Aysgarth Station Bond Issue, which raised £200,000. Throughout 1998 WRA volunteers restored the site and took over running the holiday cottage that had been created from the waiting rooms and booking office by a previous owner. The WRA, under the auspices of its WR Company arm, also acquired the $10\frac{1}{4}$ inch Pilgrim Steam Railway. The Pilgrim, which is the largest known portable railway in the U.K., is currently based at Leeming Bar station. However, it is intended to relocate the Pilgrim and operate this live steam railway between Redmire and Castle Bolton each summer until the standard gauge line is re-laid. Another major opportunity arose when the former Leyburn Station site became available. The WRA leapt at the chance and leased the site. The former station office houses the well-stocked WRA

Keith Cameron, WRA Chairman, and Jerry Swift, Network Rail Project Manager, with the train staff at the handover on 12 May 2003. (Peter Shaw)

shop that, until October 2000, had been located in the centre of Leyburn. Other parts of the building have been modified to accommodate the ticket office and café. During 2000 the Wensleydale Railway purchased the Leeming Bar station site which included the station building, former goods shed and the station master's house with existing tenants. In 2001, with some valuable help from the Territorial Army, important construction work was undertaken at Leeming Bar.

Since its inception in 1990, the WRA has welcomed the opportunities for publicity from special excursion and other trains on the line such as the train that carried water pipes in 1998 for Yorkshire Water's £4 million pipe-laying project. Further, in the absence of a railway, at different times the WRA has provided bus links from Garsdale into Wensleydale and adjacent areas for the benefit for tourists and locals alike. These have included an open-topped double-decker bus and, a first for a rural area, low-floor easy-access buses which ran the whole of the Garsdale-Northallerton route, seven days a week. In addition, the Association ran a 'Nightclub Bus' to enable local young people to enjoy the nightlife in nearby towns and, in the mid-1990s, organised helicopter flights from Castle Bolton.

November 2000 witnessed a momentous step for the WRA when it was decided to establish the Wensleydale Railway plc (Public Limited Company) to own, operate, maintain and promote the railway. The initial share offer was of 2,500,000 £1 shares. In order for this bid to be successful there had to be an initial take-up of 50,000 £1 shares by January 2001. The response was outstanding and by April 450,000 shares had been taken up. The £770,000 level was reached in October 2001 and by autumn 2003 over £1.2 million had been raised.

The creation of the plc ushered in a new era for the Wensleydale Railway and renewed hopes for achieving the aim of reinstating the services over the whole of the 40-mile line. In addition to its property and trackbed portfolio and initiatives such as the Aysgarth holiday cottage, Leyburn and Leeming Bar shops, and the Northallerton Station Kiosk, the Wensleydale Railway now owns, or has on loan, a significant amount of rolling stock and other equipment including three three-car DMU Class trains plus two Class 31 and one class 37 locomotives. The whole project is further aided by the WRA and its 3200-plus members. The WRA is able to give financial support by making grants available for acquisitions and works. Members often help as volunteers in the restoration work and some also provide additional funds by making donations or bequests.

As the millennium was ushered in the project moved forward in leaps and bounds. In 2001 the Health and Safety Executive (HSE) gave its approval in principle for the use by the Wensleydale Company of RegioSprinter light rail trains on the line once other health and safety regulations had been met. Prior to the HSE decision the WRA had, in 2000, successfully gained an agreement in principle from Railtrack for a 99-year lease of the Redmire

(Top) Ruth Annison, WRA Secretary & Marketing Director of Wensleydale Railway plc, and Roger Sonley, driver of the first train. (Peter Shaw)

(Lower) Scott Handley, Chief Executive of Wensleydale Railway plc, in the driver's cab, 4 July 2003.
(WRA collection)

Branch line from Northallerton to Redmire (including some station buildings and other structures). The draft contract was drawn up in June 2001. However, with the demise of Railtrack (which was superseded by Network Rail) the completion was delayed and the contract was not ratified until 2003.The licences were eventually received by the plc on 28 April 2003. One of the reasons for the extended delay was that the executives of the national rail network had never handed over responsibility of an active part of the country's rail system to such a small company. Although the official date for the transfer of the Redmire Branch to Wensleydale Railway plc was Monday 12 May 2003, the ceremony to mark the handover took place on Friday 6 June 2003. The celebration was attended by over 150 people and included a jazz band and a flypast by RAF Leeming. Once the Company was handed the 'key' to the railway in the form of the Branch Line Token (or staff), it moved quickly both to give route training to its drivers and to build platforms so that the passenger service could be up and running without further delay. A scheduled service timetable was announced for the summer/autumn with special trains running at weekends over the winter. Until the reconnection of the branch at Northallerton mainline station and the upgrade of the Redmire platform are

(Top) Crowds welcoming the first train at Leeming Bar. (Arthur Hartley)

(Lower) The first train being greeted at Leyburn station. (WRA Collection)

completed, the initial service has been scheduled to run between Leeming Bar (near the A1) and Leyburn.

First Scheduled Passenger Service: July - 31 October 2003

Leeming Bar dep.	10.30	12.30	14.30	16.30
Leyburn arr.	11.15	13.15	15.15	17.15
Leyburn dep.	11.30	13.30	15.30	17.30
Leeming Bar arr.	12.15	14.15	16.15	18.15

The first trains ran on 4 July 2003 and so on that day, amid great excitement, the WRA achieved one of its major short-term objectives. Extra trains were run on the day to ensure that all prospective passengers could travel on the newly opened line. As with the opening of the first part of the original railway in 1877, crowds lined stations along the route and church bells were rung in celebration. Teams of bell ringers from all over North Yorkshire, led by David Town of All Saints Church, Northallerton, rang bells at a total of 14 churches in sequence up Wensleydale to mark the passage of the first train. The DMU Class 107 had departed from Leeming Bar promptly at 10.30 a.m. and was full of people who had paid £95 for the special first day commemorative Rover ticket. A strong national and local media presence ensured that all the major television channels and radio stations carried the story of the reopening. Former Leader of the Conservative Party, William Hague MP, gave the go ahead for the commencement of the service by waving the green flag. David Bowe, the local MEP, and Christopher Awdry, WRA patron, travelled on the first day train. Actor Robert Hardy, a loyal and active patron of the WRA, sent a letter offering his congratulations but also his apologies that he was 'extremely disappointed' not to be able to make the opening day.

Other celebrations were to follow. On 5 March 2004 the new railway received a royal visitor, HRH the Duke of York. Prince Andrew travelled on board the DMU Class 107 from Leeming Bar to Leyburn station where he unveiled a commemorative plaque. The fiftieth anniversary of the last through train was marked on 24 April 2004 by a commemorative train. Among the passengers were ten people who travelled on the last train in 1954 including the fireman, Derick Appleton. In addition to the celebrations much work has been undertaken. Passing loops have been

William Hague, MP and former Conservative Party Leader, waving the green flag for the commencement of the new passenger service on 4 July 2003.
(Peter Shaw)

constructed at Bedale and Constable Burton and run-round loops at Leeming Bar and Leyburn. A new temporary station will shortly be completed at Northallerton and the Redmire platform will be upgraded. This will enable a two-train scheduled service to run over the full twenty-two miles from Northallerton to Redmire for the first time since 1954. In order to ensure that the Wensleydale railway journey is as full as possible, link buses will be run at peak periods where necessary, for example between Leyburn and Aysgarth.

Much work remains to be done and, in order to help finance the next phase, a second share offer for £2.75 million has been agreed. As soon as the whole of the Northallerton to Redmire section is operational, the remainder of the line will be reinstated in stages. The Hawes to Garsdale reinstatement and the connection to the Settle-Carlisle line remains a priority. However, as with the struggle to get the original railway built, it will be a few years yet before, once again after half a century of silence, a scheduled passenger service runs the full length of Wensleydale.

Sources

PUBLIC RECORD OFFICE: Documents relating to the Midland, N.E.R. and L.N.E.R. Companies, returns of the Ministry of Agriculture, Fisheries and Food – Public Health (Dairies) Bill 1882; Census Information 1891, 1901.

HOUSE OF LORDS RECORD OFFICE: Documents relating to proposed railways.

NORTH YORKSHIRE COUNTY RECORD OFFICE: Documents relating to proposed railways; Census abstracts 1801-1951.

NORTH YORKSHIRE COUNTY LIBRARY HEADQUARTERS; Census Enumerators' Handbooks 1861-1881.

PRIVATELY-HELD DOCUMENTS: Garth Day Books; Documents relating to the N.E.R. and L.N.E.R. Companies.

NEWSPAPERS: *The Wensleydale Advertiser; Richmond and Ripon Chronicle; The Bedale and Northallerton Times; Darlington and Stockton Times.*

DIRECTORIES OF THE NORTH RIDING OF YORKSHIRE: Kelly – 1857; White – 1867; Kelly – 1872; Bulmer – 1890; Kelly – 1893.

Hardcastle G. - *Wanderings in Wensleydale (1864)*
Late Hardcastle G. - *Wanderings in Wensleydale (Revised by C. Horner, 1884)*
Jackson J. - *Handbook for Tourists in Yorkshire and Complete History of the County (1891)*

Leyland J. - *Wensleydale and Swaledale Guide (c.1896)*
Murray J. - *Handbook for Travellers in Yorkshire (1882)*
Routh J. - *Guide to Wensleydale (1878)*
Speight H. - *Romantic Richmondshire (1897)*
Spencer G. - *Guide to Swaledale and Arkengarthdale (c.1905)*
Ward J. - *Methodism in Swaledale (1865)*
Whaley C. - *History of Askrigg (1899)*
Whellen T. - *History and Topography of the City of York and the North Riding of Yorkshire (1857)*
Baughan P. - *The Railways of Wharfedale (1969)*
Countryside Commission - *Dales Rail (1979)*
Deane P. & Cole W. A. - *British Economic Growth 1688-1959 (1962)*
Goode C. T. - *The Wensleydale Branch (1980)*
Grundy J. - *The Origins of Liverpool Cowkeepers (unpublished thesis, Lancaster 1982)*
Hartley M. & Ingilby J. - *Wensleydale (1936)*
- *Yorkshire Village (1953)*
Harwood Long W.- *A Survey of Agriculture in Yorkshire (1969)*
Hoole K. - *Railways in the Yorkshire Dales (1975)*
Houghton F. & Foster W. - *The Story of the Settle-Carlisle Line (1965)*
Parris H. W. - *Railways in the Northern Pennines (unpublished thesis, Leeds, 1954)*

The author

Until her retirement in December 2001, Dr. Christine Hallas was Dean of Arts and Social Sciences at Trinity and All Saints College, University of Leeds. She is continuing her association with the College as an Honorary Research Fellow. In 1988 she completed research for her Ph.D. thesis into social and economic change in nineteenth century Wensleydale and Swaledale. A major part of the research centred on the impact of transport, particularly rail, in the area. She has since written on many aspects of dales life including self help, poverty, the lead and textile industries, migration, farming, and craft occupations.

Acknowledgments

Many people have provided material for this book and, as far as possible, acknowledgments of individuals are listed below. In addition, I should like to thank the staff of the Public Record Office, the House of Lords Record Office, the North Yorkshire County Record Office, the North Yorkshire County Library headquarters, the Yorkshire Dales National Park Department, the *Darlington and Stockton Times* and Ackrill Newspaper Ltd. Further, I should particularly like to thank Marie Hartley and the late Joan Ingilby for their encouragement and advice and late Kenneth A. Bell for his time and patience in assisting me to decipher certain documents. Finally, the book would not have been written without the help and support of my husband who also proof read the text.

My thanks to the following for their assistance including the loan of documents: M. Aslin, L. Barker, M. Bell, K. Bergurud, T.C. Calvert, E. Daykin, D. Hall, R. Hugill, M. Kirby, N. McDougall, P. Moore, H.W. Pearson, D.F. Severs, A.V. Slack, G. Smith, R. Tyson, M. Weatherald, A. Weddle. My thanks are also due to the WRA members, Ruth Annison, Scott Handley and, particularly, Michael Bentley, for their assistance with the final chapter of this latest edition of The Wensleydale Railway.

Further Reading

Additional reading about social and economic change in Wensleydale including statistics on the Wensleydale railway can be found in C.S. Hallas, 'The Social and Economic Impact of a Rural Railway: The Wensleydale line' *Agricultural History Review*, 34, 1986; - *Rural Responses to Industrialisation: The North Yorkshire Pennines 1790-1914,* Bern, 1999; - *In Sickness and in Health: Askrigg Equitable, Benevolent, and Friendly Society 1809-2000*, York, 2000.

The student who is interested in track layout and other technical details should refer to C.T. Goode – *The Wensleydale branch*, Locomotion Papers, 1980 and S.C.Jenkins, *History of the Wensleydale Branch*, Oakwood Press, 1993. For a pictorial history see T. Eaton, *Memories of the Wensleydale Railway*, 2003.

WENSLEYDALE RAILWAY.
The UK's longest privately-operated standard gauge line

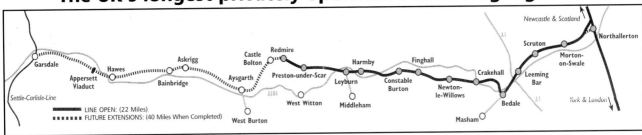

THE RAILWAY IS BEING RE-OPENED IN 4 STAGES: 1. NORTHALLERTON-REDMIRE. 2. REDMIRE-CASTLE BOLTON-AYSGARTH. 3. GARSDALE-HAWES. 4. HAWES-AYSGARTH.

When in Wensleydale why not visit our shops situated at Leyburn, Leeming Bar and (soon) Bedale Stations. As well as being able to learn the latest news of developments along the Railway you are able to browse in our well stocked sales areas. We stock a very large range of books, videos, gifts and other merchandise related to the Wensleydale Railway and the Yorkshire Dales. There are also many other railway and transport items – plus Thomas The Tank Engine for the children.

SHOPS AND RETAIL ENQUIRIES (ONLY) TO:
LEYBURN STATION
Harmby Road, Leyburn DL8 5ET
Tel: 01969 625182

LEEMING BAR STATION
Leases Road, Leeming Bar, DL7 9AR
Tel: 01677 425805

BEDALE STATION
(to be announced)

The Wensleydale Railway Association was formed in 1990 to investigate the feasibility of returning passenger trains to Wensleydale. From small beginnings the Association has grown to be a major organisation in the field of Britain's independent railways with some 3500 members.

With the formation of Wensleydale Railway plc the WRA adopted the role of a supporting organisation providing the framework for members to keep in touch with developments and to take an active role in working with and for the Railway, should they wish.

Why not become a WRA member and supporter of the Railway by joining now? You will receive our magazine RELAY and other regular information.

You can join up at one of our shops or write for an application form to:
W.R.A., P.O. Box 65, Northallerton, DL7 8YZ.

Wensleydale Railway plc was launched in 2000 by the Wensleydale Railway Association for the purpose of owning and operating the railway and associated traffic infrastructure in the Dale, the initial share issue raising £1.2 million.

This huge success paved the way for a grand re-opening of the first section of the line in July 2003, following transfer of the leasehold interest from Network Rail's predecessor, Railtrack.

You now have an opportunity to invest in this unique and exciting project. For more information and up to date news on developments, visit our website at: www.wensleydalerailway.com
or write for a Share Prospectus to:
Wensleydale Railway plc,
35 High Street, Northallerton, DL7 8EE

The share prospectus is also available by Freephone on 0500 824166 (office hours) and from:

Wensleydale Railway plc, Freepost NEA 10812, Northallerton, North Yorkshire, DL7 9BR
(no stamp required)

TICKET, TIMETABLE & GENERAL ENQUIRIES: 08454 505474